CU00661291

EVERYONE HAS A STORY

13 REAL-LIFE SHORT STORIES ABOUT LOVE, LOSS, SURVIVAL, AND PERSEVERANCE

MEMOIR VOL. 1

JOSEPH BOGLINO

WWW.WELOVETHATSTORY.COM

Copyright © 2021 Joseph Boglino. All rights reserved.

The content contained within this book may not be reproduced, duplicated, or transmitted without direct written permission from the author or the publisher.

Under no circumstances will any blame or legal responsibility be held against the publisher, or author, for any damages, reparation, or monetary loss due to the information contained within this book, either directly or indirectly. You are responsible for your own choices, actions, and results.

Legal Notice:

This book is copyright protected. This book is only for personal use. You cannot amend, distribute, sell, use, quote, or paraphrase any part, or the content within this book, without the consent of the author or publisher.

Disclaimer Notice:

Please note the information contained within this document is for educational and entertainment purposes only. All effort has been executed to present accurate, up-to-date, and reliable, complete information. No warranties of any kind are declared or implied. Readers acknowledge that the author is not engaging in the rendering of legal, financial, medical, or professional advice. The content within this book has been derived from various sources. Please consult a licensed professional before attempting any techniques outlined in this book.

By reading this document, the reader agrees that under no circumstances is the author responsible for any losses, direct or indirect, which are incurred as a result of the use of the information contained within this document, including, but not limited to, errors, omissions, or inaccuracies.

CONTENTS

TELL YOUR STORY

WWW.WELOVETHATSTORY.COM

Tell us your story

What is the one story that has defined your life?
If you would like to tell it, we are here to write it.
This service is entirely **FREE**. All we want to do is
share it with the world!

STEP ONE

Tell us who you are and how to contact you

Name:
Email:
Phone:
When is the best time to contact you:

STEP TWO

Title and Short Description

If you were to give your story a title, what would it
be:

Provide a brief description of your story:

STEP THREE

Send your information

Email to jboglino@welovethatstory.com

THERE IS NO CHARGE FOR THIS SERVICE. YOU WILL RECEIVE
YOUR STORY IN A WRITTEN FORMAT, AND IT MAY BE CHOSEN
FOR ONE OF OUR SUBSEQUENT PUBLICATIONS TO SHARE WITH
THE WORLD. WE ONLY ASK THAT YOU SIGN A RELEASE TO LET
US PUBLISH YOUR STORY.

To Dad, for inspiring me about people, life, and your stories. And to Mom, your constant encouragement and your interest in collecting stories and telling the tales inspired me to put pen to paper.

To all the people vulnerable enough to share their stories so the rest of us can be inspired and learn from the impactful events of their lives. Thank you.

History, despite its wrenching pain, cannot be unlived; but if faced with courage, need not be lived again.

— MAYA ANGELOU

INTRODUCTION

Charlene's twin sister was murdered in cold blood in front of her children. Vivian survived a dangerous escape from Vietnam. Angel lived with two ghosts she thought were real. Meg fought for an abusive marriage, lost, and then found the love of her life. When Jerry lost his phone, he found a wife. Barry slept on his ex-wife's couch for eight years, caring for her as she battled Parkinson's. A villager protecting the town told Irina to flee and to take nothing but her life.

Real-life stories from real people. Stories filled with tragedies, heartbreak, happiness, love, forgiveness, and compassion. It's incredible what people go through in their lives, and when they share their tales, we feel connected, impacted, and honored.

This book is about thirteen people faced with very different challenges that changed their lives forever and shaped who they are today. These defining moments demonstrate extraordinary courage that will inspire and teach. Told by people from ages 21 to 75 years old, these stories reveal lives confronted with tough decisions, most of which were made selflessly, and there is a story for every reader. These short stories—slivers of people's lives—will make you laugh, cry, and be inspired.

We Love That Story is all about telling stories from real people around the world, using their experiences to share relatable and inspiring encounters. Stories help us connect. Stories help us understand. Stories can teach us valuable lessons while giving us insight into how other people dealt with an event, a situation, or a decision.

Everyone has a story. It doesn't matter what life we have lived, what we have experienced, or what we have gone through—we all have a story to tell. What's your story?

If you are interested in telling it, let us know. We would be more than happy to sit with you, listen, and be your voice. Contact us at jboglino@welovethatstory.com. We would be honored for the opportunity to share your story with the world.

Now, get ready for thirteen short stories that will take you to the front row of courage, love, tragedy, and mystery.

CHAPTER 1: FORGIVENESS IS LIKE A MIRACLE

"I remember dropping the phone and just crying, just screaming. I lost it! People were in the hotel lobby just staring at me. I didn't care. I've never experienced anything like that in my life, and I was devastated!"

When Charlene phoned her family from a payphone in a seedy California hotel to check in on how they were doing, she got the news that would change her life forever.

"Snow killed Charlotte!"

Charlene's twin sister, Charlotte, had been killed. She was murdered by Charlotte's estranged second husband, Leslie, also known as "Snow." It was 1974. The twins were 28 years old.

The night before Charlene received the news, Leslie had come looking for Charlotte at her apartment. She wasn't home. Charlotte's daughter refused Leslie entry and called her mom to warn her not to come home because Leslie's erratic behavior was reminiscent of prior violent encounters. Leslie stayed outside, pacing and waiting.

"Charlotte had attended a drug rehab meeting, and her first husband was driving her back home. When they drove up to the house, Leslie shot both of them in the car. My sister died instantly. Her first husband later recovered."

Charlotte's kids were now without a mother. Charlotte's youngest child, a baby boy she had with Leslie, was just ten months old.

"When you're born with someone, you don't see how you could live life without them...like a twin sister. And then I thought about the babies she had, and I cried."

Charlene had taken a trip from Colorado to California with Jack, whom she had met the month before in her neighborhood. Charlene and her family rarely ventured out on a big vacation out of state. It was her chance to travel and take a break from raising four children of her own.

"I always wanted to travel, and this was an opportunity for a poor, divorced mother to go somewhere. I remember my grandmother told me not to go. She never wanted me to have any kind of freedom. While dropping my daughter off, even Charlotte warned, 'You know that guy could get you right outside of town and kill you.'

"I was kind of like a flower child, as they call it. I was raising my children but still having some fun and trying to make the best of life. So, when this guy said he was going to California, I wanted to go. I had never been anywhere. I was still very young, being that I married so young, and I was still finding my way. Even though I had these children to raise, I felt I was living my life the best I knew how."

Charlene was in Oakland when she called home that fateful morning. She was excited to tell her family how much she had seen and check in on the kids.

"Are you by yourself," her mother asked the moment she answered Charlene's call. The hotel Charlene was in didn't have phones in the guest rooms. She was calling from a payphone in the hotel lobby.

"I don't know how long I was down there, but I went back up to the room and told Jack, 'I got to go. My sister has been killed!'"

"I don't think I'll let you go," Jack said.

"My children need me, and her children need me, too," Charlotte replied in disbelief.

Charlene, scared to fly, called her father to buy her a train ticket back to Denver.

"I kept thinking this was just not real. I just couldn't believe it. But it was real, and when I got home, I never have felt such devastation in all my life. There was a point where I thought I didn't want to live anymore without my sister. It just didn't seem like I should be here. She wasn't here!"

But it had happened. The family was devastated, and there was Charlotte's baby boy without a mother or a father.

"You know that evening when she was killed, I got the most horrible pain right in the middle of my chest. It was this unexplainable quick, sharp pain. I'll never forget it. I just didn't know what it was. I still don't, but they tell me that one of those bullets went straight to her heart and killed her instantly. That pain was the pain that I felt. It was a pain that I had never felt ever before in my life and have never felt again."

Charlene and her sister shared the same number and sex ratio of children: three boys and a girl. The family now had to decide what they were going to do with Charlotte's children.

"At the time, I wasn't sure if I would have to raise the three oldest because their dad was in the hospital and not in very good shape after sustaining multiple gunshot wounds. I considered that I might have to take all of them, but once he got better, he was able to take his own three children, and I took the baby. He was only ten months old, and of course he needed someone to care for him. I was the next person in line that would be appropriate to do that. I just moved right in and became his mother.

"I was the one because nobody wanted to take care of a murderer's child. They didn't want to constantly be reminded of the murderer when looking into the eyes of an innocent child. I didn't even give it a second thought. I just knew that I was the one to do it."

The baby's name was Leslie. The same name as his father.

Charlene never formally adopted Leslie Jr. She didn't have to. She just assumed her new role and "took it day by day." When it was time to enroll him in school or take him to a doctor's appointment, Charlene was never questioned about biological parentage. However, when it was time to get a birth certificate, she had a decision to make. Was she to keep his name—her sister's murderer's name—or would she change it?

"I really couldn't change his name because my sister said that his name was going to be "Leslie" like his father. Later on, I thought I could change his name, but at that moment, it was not an option for me. I had nothing to do with choosing his name, and I certainly wasn't going to punish him by not naming him what his mother had wanted."

Leslie Jr. began to call Charlene "mom," and she set out to treat and raise him as if he were her own. There wasn't much talk about what happened and who Leslie Sr. was. He was just a part of the family. Charlene knew that there would come a time when she would tell him about what happened to his mother and father, but she thought she would wait until he was older to understand better. Unfortunately, one of Charlene's family members had other plans.

"A family member decided that, for whatever reason, she had to tell Leslie that I wasn't his mom. The family member was very special in my heart, so I was very shocked that she would reveal that! I was going to tell him in time—but in my time, not in their time. But because she said that, I suddenly wasn't his mom. I mean, it took everything for me even to see myself as his mom; it just devastated me. I then had to tell a five-year-old the story of what happened. I wasn't ready, but I didn't want him to think that I deceived him in any way. So, I sat him down, and I told him. I don't even know if he had a response, but at least I told him and was glad I did. His response was not what an older child or an older person would be. Sometimes when you're young, I think the reality of life and death doesn't become real to you until much later when you see yourself losing people that you love. I don't think he understood it. "

While it wasn't instantaneous for Charlene to be able to see herself as his mother, it was less of a journey for the rest of the family. Charlene's other children accepted their new brother right away. Their families had frequently spent time together before Charlotte's passing.

"We were close. Some of my kids might be at Charlotte's house, and some of hers would be at my house. Brothers and sisters and cousins, all together. In fact, my mother, sister, and I had children that were almost the same age. We were all bearing children at the same time. It sounds crazy, but my mother was only fourteen when my twin sister and I were born. So she was still in her childbearing years while we were having children. My grandmother thought it was just a disgrace. She would shake her head and growl, 'All of you having babies at the same time.' She thought it was terrible. But yes, my children were well aware of what had taken place, and they embraced him."

Five years after Charlene's life had changed forever, and around the same time she was forced to tell Leslie Jr. the story about his parents, Charlene was on duty at the Admissions Office at University Hospital when she heard a voice say, "Hi Charlene." Charlene turned, and it was the man that had killed her sister: her former bother-in-law, Leslie Sr.

"He was already out of prison! At that moment, I was speechless. I'm surprised I didn't faint because it was just a shock to me to turn and see him. While I had forgiven him in my heart, I was face-to-face with him now and didn't know what to do. I had to, at that moment, make a decision. How would I handle this? I didn't say that I forgave him, because I had already written and told him so. What I did do was offer to let him see his child. I always thought that since I didn't get any paperwork, I didn't adopt him. I have nothing legally to tie him to me. I only tied him to my heart. So I asked, 'Would you like to see your son?' That's the only thing that made sense to me. I thought that maybe he could rectify the situation if he would get to know his son and raise him the rest of the way."

Leslie accepted Charlene's offer.

"I got such flak from my family; it was just unbearable. But I felt like I was doing the right thing. Nobody agreed with the fact that I allowed him to see his child. I couldn't erase the fact that he was his father. I didn't think my family would be as angry with me as they were, but once I decided I would do it, it didn't matter what anyone felt about it. I was just going to do what I thought was the right thing to do."

Charlene's offer to Leslie Sr. to see his son was instinctual. Based on everything she believed in and what she learned through her deep faith, she had a choice to make. She thought that the rest of her family felt the same way she did about forgiveness. Unfortunately for Charlene, her family was strongly opposed to the thought of forgiveness in this case. They were angry at her for even thinking about allowing Leslie Jr. to meet a 'murderer.' Charlene thought it was an opportunity to make something good out of a terrible event.

"I saw that a horrible thing had been done, but there was still hope that some good come out of it. Leslie Sr. could embrace and raise his son and give him a good life. I had been able to separate his horrible act from him as a person in order to make a decision that I thought would be best for all concerned. His anger had been directed at my sister, but I didn't think that included his son. I am not saying it is right, but I felt that he could still love his son, and he could be repentant."

Charlene and Leslie Sr. arranged for the meeting. When Leslie Sr. arrived at Charlene's house, he came with a woman. She was his new wife, and she was pregnant.

"I allowed him to see his son hoping that Leslie would decide he wanted to take him and raise him. I don't know why I thought that. That never happened. It was clear that the new wife, pregnant with her own kid, didn't want to start her married life raising a stepchild. So, what I intended never happened. Actually, you know, she ended up having twins! I mean, unbelievable!"

The meeting between father and son was uneventful. Leslie Jr. went out to play with his brothers and sisters shortly after the introduction.

To this day, even in the face of all the criticism from her family, Charlene does not regret making the offer. Her strong belief in forgiveness and taking actions over words has always been at the core of her behavior. Leslie Jr., now in his 40s, still has difficulties reconciling what his father did, but he is grateful for his "auntie," who stepped up to raise and love a child that was not hers. He calls Charlene to talk about his mother and tells her that he does have a relationship of sorts with his father. She can tell in his voice that he struggles with never knowing his mother.

"We all say that we would 'forgive,' but when the time comes, we often fall short of actually doing it. To me, it's not just a word to say. I believe in keeping my word. My offer was a combination of doing the best thing for the child and a desire that this would be an opportunity for Leslie Sr. to repent for what he had done. I didn't get to this decision right away. I was furious when it happened, but enough time had passed that I could exercise what I believe was the right action."

Charlene's decision to forgive her sister's murderer has played a significant role in her life and shaped who she is, but it has not been easy.

"Forgiveness didn't come immediately. I had some other intentions before that, and they weren't good either. I'm a person of faith, but I wasn't so strong in my faith. My life has always been to please my God, but of course, I've fallen short of that many times. Vengeance crossed my mind. That was my first feeling. Set up some plan to get this man back for what he had done to my sister. But in the process of living my life and raising my children, it didn't make very good sense to me after a short while. So, when I first saw him again that day at University Hospital, it was like there was no other sensible thing to do for me than to practice what I genuinely believe, and that was forgiveness. Forgiveness is like a miracle. It's just something that works. It works for the person that forgives. I felt that, for my own sake, I didn't want to live my life in bitterness. That's not who I wanted to be.

"Losing my sister was the most traumatic thing in my life. But as a result of that event, I became stronger. You can either let them make you or break you. That's how I see it. I think I became a better person, not immediately, but in time because it made me appreciate aging. I didn't dread it like some people do because I thought about my sister. She was only 28. I've been given all this time, so I don't begrudge aging due to that. And I think that's a good thing. I always appreciate that I've been given a whole life. She didn't even see all her kids grow up. That was a benchmark for me to measure a lot of my life by.

"I keep seeing this better person coming out as a result of traumatic or difficult times in my life. You would never choose for these things to happen, but the fact that I went through it and survived made me a better person on the other side of it. Strangely, it's almost worth what I've been through because I see that not only am I a better person, but I can help other people. When I can help somebody else, it gives a little more meaning to my life. Because when you're better, you can help make somebody else a little bit better, too."

CHAPTER 2: TWO FAMILIES BOUND BY FATE, LOVE, AND TRAGEDY

*M*arysia and John have been married for more than twenty-five years. They currently live in Chicago, but their connection began many decades ago in Poland when Marysia was still in her mother's womb, and John's mother was grieving the tragic death of her daughter. One mother consoling the other. These families were forever intertwined at that moment, supporting each other in that heartbreaking moment and in tragedies to come.

John's oldest sister Margaret was crushed to death at just 7 years old. She was reaching for a cookie on the top shelf of a bookcase when it tumbled over on top of her.

Marysia's sister, Ela, died from lung cancer when she was 23 years old. What made her death so shocking was that she had never smoked a day or lived in an environment with bad air quality.

Ela had complained for months about nausea, and coupled with several fainting spells, she was worried about what was causing these symptoms. She went to see several doctors. Because of her age and relatively healthy-looking appearance, not one doctor took her concerns seriously and found nothing wrong with her. One doctor incredulously told her that he thought she was faking her illness to get out of work. Their ambivalence and lack of empathy mystified Ela and her husband. Repeatedly they hit a wall in their search for a remedy.

What was Ela to do? One morning, while getting ready for work, she had another fainting spell, and her husband, Paul, took her directly to the emergency room. This time he chose a hospital referred to them by a friend who knew the director. This concerned and proactive professional provided the intervention needed to get Ela the care, attention, and testing that ultimately diagnosed a genuine issue; the test results stunned everyone.

"When they looked at Ela's X-ray images, it looked like someone had scattered sand all over her lungs. Each grain of sand was a seed of cancer. It was everywhere. The results also showed that the cancer had spread to her brain. She never left the hospital," her sister Marysia said. "They told us that it was the type of cancer that usually occurs in older men who were heavy smokers. We couldn't believe it."

The family was told that the cancer was rare in young women and that she had only six to eight months to live—a devastating expiration date.

Marysia had been preparing for her wedding to her fiancé, John, well before the terrible news of Ela's diagnosis. Marysia wanted to cancel all plans. How was she going to get married without her sister being there? How would she celebrate her marriage while her sister lay in a hospital bed fighting for her life?

"Ela told me that I couldn't cancel my wedding because of her. She wouldn't hear of it. It was so difficult to move forward with my wedding with her so sick."

Marysia and Ela were very close siblings. They shared everything. Ela was a role model, and they loved each other deeply. Marysia and John would hang out with Ela and her husband all the time. They took vacations, spent holidays with one another, and dreamed of raising families together. The four of them were inseparable.

Ela and Paul wouldn't make the wedding that summer. The chemotherapy treatments at the hospital were so invasive and devastating to Ela's health that there was no way they could attend. They were too busy fighting for Ela's life. Even with the valiant fight that Ela had put up, she died five months after the diagnosis.

The day after the funeral, Marysia and her family were in mourning. After a restless night, Marysia, staying at her in-laws' house, went down to the kitchen to get breakfast. Monika, John's sister, was there too. Monika was troubled and had something to tell Marysia. She was hesitant to say anything about what was bothering her out of respect for the terrible situation. Still, she felt compelled to share a dream she had had about Marysia's deceased sister.

"Monika looked anxious. I asked her what was wrong. She broke down and told me of a 'weird' dream she had the night before where she saw herself wearing a white wedding dress holding a beautiful bouquet standing over Ela's casket. She said it looked like she was getting married, but all the people around were dressed in black waiting for a funeral."

Monika was John's youngest sister who was not in any serious relationship at the time of the funeral and was certainly not planning any wedding. A 'weird' dream that seemed like she was at her wedding and standing over the grave of her brother's future sister-in-law greatly unnerved her. How could she have such a dream amid such loss?

Marysia didn't give much thought to the dream. While it was 'weird,' it was just a dream. Perhaps Monika had been significantly affected by her own sister's death. She chalked it up as a unique vision and nothing more. No one spoke of it again. But was it a sign of things to come?

Like most people who experience such a close and devastating loss, Marysia was equally distressed and angry.

"When Ela died, I complained to God all the time. I was so upset. Even though we were very close, we were very different. I was considered the 'problem child' at home. My mother always compared me to Ela and told me to be more like her. I couldn't understand why it happened to the better sister! Why did he take her away and not me? She was smart and ambitious, perfect and kind. I didn't feel like I was as good as she. I didn't deserve to be alive and to be here without her.

"I remember one particular day being completely consumed by grief as I sat in one of the two armchairs in my living room. It was a beautiful, sunny day. Bright, natural light filled the room. The windows were open, and I watched the breeze gently blow the white, sheer curtains into the room. It looked so peaceful. It was like a daydream, and it was so vivid. My sister walked out from behind the curtain. She looked very healthy and had a smile on her face. She sat down on the other armchair next to me. I wasn't shocked. It was all very easy, very peaceful. I turned to her and asked her where she came from? She answered me by taking my hands and looked straight into my eyes. 'I had to come. I left you, but what would you have done if you had been in my place?' I asked her why she would ask me such a question? She asked another question. 'Would you like to continue living with such horrible cancer in your body? You wouldn't be able to have kids with your husband, and every year, wrought by fear, you would be retested and have to wait to see if cancer returned. Tell me, what would you choose if you were in that situation?' I just looked at her and said, 'You are right. I would want to die too.' From that moment, I had no remorse or guilt about my sister's death. I knew she was at peace. Because of that conversation, I am not afraid to die. If I die tomorrow, I am okay with it. I have no fear of death."

A year after Ela's death, Marysia and John decided to immigrate to the U.S. The move was a big decision for them, but they both just wanted a change of scenery. Everything around them reminded them of Ela. While Marysia had found her peace with her sister's passing, it was still very heartbreaking. They thought they would get a fresh start in a foreign place far away from their home in Poland.

Paul, Ela's widow, and Monika, John's sister, drove Marysia and John to the airport. Marysia and John were excited for what lay before them but solemn, knowing that they were leaving their friends and family behind. They were going to miss them all, but they knew that the opportunities in the U.S. were something that they could not let pass them by. They said their good-byes to Paul and Monika and set their sights on Chicago.

"After we left for the U.S., we learned that Paul and Monika had started going out together! A couple of years later they got married! The dream that she had told me about in the kitchen the day after the funeral turned out to be a premonition! I couldn't believe it. I was happy for them both. Now, the dream makes sense."

Paul went from being Marysia's brother-in-law to John's. Paul and Monika have been married for over twenty years and have two kids.

Marysia and John both lost sisters tragically. From the day Marysia's mother consoled John's mother over Margaret's accident, the families have shared personal tragedies, but, in each case, the families were there for one another.

CHAPTER 3: DON'T TAKE ANYTHING WITH YOU BUT YOUR LIFE

By the time the Nazi German forces reached Irina's village in eastern Poland in 1939, the Russian Army and the Ukrainian Army had already occupied the village. The former had taken anything of value; the latter had arrested and sent Irina's father—along with all the town's teachers, police, and politicians—to Siberia. Irina's father's crime was merely owning hunting rifles; he was not a part of any resistance. He was just a father of five children, three boys and two girls, who kept a farm and hunted to put food on the table for his family. Irina was just 13 years old.

The village was Huta Stefańska, a Polish town founded in the seventeenth century. In 1939, it had about one thousand inhabitants. While it doesn't exist anymore, it was located approximately 120 miles east of the current Polish-Ukrainian border. All houses inhabited by the Poles were burned to the ground in

1943 after local Ukrainians stole all their possessions. What remains today is a cross with the Polish inscription: Jezu Ratuj Nas (Jesus Save Us).

Between 1939 and 1943, Irina's village was primarily lawless, caught between Russian, Ukrainian, and German armies. Since all police and intelligencia were sent away to Siberia, the Ukrainian Army provided much of the law enforcement. However, their enforcement subjected Poles to constant attack, looting, and murder.

Irina recalls one day when a group of Ukrainian soldiers came to her family's house. They had a Jewish woman in their custody. The Ukrainian officer told her mother to watch the woman, warning that if she escaped while under her mother's watch, he would come back and kill the entire family. Irina's mother stayed up nervous and terrified all night, afraid that the sleeping woman in their kitchen might try to escape from the house. The Ukrainian police came the following day and took her to the police station. Irina heard that the woman escaped by bribing the police officers watching her. She never knew what happened to the woman after that.

During those lawless four years, Irina rarely saw soldiers from any of the armies in the area. Huta Stefańska was just a tiny village tucked out of the way of most military activity. So, when a platoon of Ukrainian soldiers did come to the village one day, everyone feared for their lives. Occasionally, the Ukrainian Army would surround the village and not let anyone in or out.

The Ukrainian Army usually did this when they had a tip from someone that Jews were hiding or being hidden by the villagers. It was a capital crime to aid or hide Jews in Poland during the war, and it meant certain death if caught. As the Ukrainian Army was grouping the villagers for questioning and possible execution, while searching for Jews, they asked the village priest if anyone was hiding Jews. They thought he would be a sympathetic contributor to their hunt. The town villagers were hiding Jews wherever they could. They would hide them in their homes, in the church, and in government buildings. When asked if there were any Jews, the priest lied and told them no. The Ukrainian Army begrudgingly believed him and left. Irina's family, part of the group rounded up by the Ukrainians, was more than relieved.

Irina remembers one day when Ukrainians attacked her village. It was the summer of 1943. The village's men told all women and children to hide within the local two-story school building. They climbed the building's stairs and stuffed pillows in the windows, supposedly so bullets wouldn't go through. Fighting began—it went on for some time, then stopped, and Irina was unsure why. Maybe the Ukrainians ran out of ammunition and went to reload? The lull in the fighting gave the villagers time to regroup. They decided they would all flee to a nearby town. Everyone gathered and began to leave, but the Ukrainians returned and started shooting again. They all ran back into the school where the men stood guard to keep the women and children safe. It started raining very hard. There was a break in the shooting again because of this. The Ukrainian army ceased the attack to find shelter and wait out the storm. The gap in the attack allowed the villagers to escape. The people who were in charge of keeping the group in the school safe took advantage of the pause in the fighting and said, "Run! Don't take anything with you but your life!" That was all, and so that's what they did. Irina didn't even have shoes on her feet. The rocks, thorns, and rough terrain through the woods on the way to the neighboring village tore Irina's feet and left her hobbling by the time they reached their destination.

They went into the rain and escaped to another village, but that village had been destroyed and burned. There was no place to go but back to the surrounding woods. They slept in the woods for days. They found a small girl hiding by herself in the twisted underbrush and took her with them. Most of the group decided to go to Rafałówka in hopes that a larger town would provide more safety and shelter. It was approximately 30 miles away. They took a train to get as far away as they could. Irina's family met someone there that they knew and stayed with them for a while. They slept on the hay upstairs in a barn for days while they determined what to do next.

While in Rafałówka, Irina remembers a moment when the Germans found a small Jewish boy. He was about 9 or 10 years old. They shot him. To this day, she remembers seeing the boy standing and then falling with the sound of a gunshot.

Irina's mother decided afterward that they had to leave. They took a coal train to a town called Rowne. Shortly after that, the people who stayed back in Rafałówka were attacked and killed by Ukrainians. Most of the victims were women and children, as a majority of the young boys and men in the town had left to serve in the Polish Army.

In Rowne, a Ukrainian family took care of Irina's family and let them stay in their attic. Eventually, Irina, her mother, her two brothers, and her sister boarded a train to Germany, forced to find safety with the enemy. Germany needed people to work on farms since most of the men were in the German army. The only family member missing was Irina's oldest brother. He was killed in 1943 in a village near Huta Stefańska.

In the summer of 1943, the Ukrainian Insurgent Army (UPA) carried out orders to ethnically cleanse Irina's birthplace, and a UPA unit razed the villages of Rafałówka and Huta Stefańska. In just two days, they destroyed the Polish colonies and the people living there. Irina's brother was killed in the conflict. While no one knows if Irina's brother was a part of the resistance, Irina remarked that her mother could not recognize him when viewing his body because only half his face was left.

"At the beginning of the war, the Russians sent my father to Siberia, and my oldest brother took over the farm. The day a Ukrainian soldier killed my brother was a regular day. I still see him the way he was—putting the horse to a little wagon. When he heard that the Ukrainians were attacking a little village nearby, he asked my mother if he could go and help them. My mother didn't want him to go, but he really wanted to. She finally said, 'Okay, go.' That was it. I believe in destiny, you know because if he hadn't gone to help other people, he would have been working the farm, and maybe he would still be alive. You never know."

When Irina's family arrived in Germany, Nazi officials separated the family, sending Irina and her sister to work at a farm near Hamburg while her mother and youngest brother were sent to a different farm. Her younger brother, Henry, was assigned to a third farm. The German woman who Irina and her sister worked for was good to them. They worked in the fields every day, were fed well, and had a warm place to sleep. Irina's brother Henry, however, was worked hard by his German family and he was rarely given any food. When Irina told the woman she was staying with about how her brother was being treated, the woman convinced authorities to move Henry to another family.

Irina worked at the farm until the end of the war. She often had to flee to a bunker nearby as Allied bombers bombed the areas near Hamburg. There were many frantic nights of getting dressed and rushing to safety when this happened. She would often see Hamburg on fire.

When the war ended, the Allied forces sent Irina and her family to a camp for displaced persons. In post-World War II Europe, these camps were established in Germany, Austria, and Italy, primarily for refugees from Eastern Europe and the former inmates of the Nazi German concentration camps. At the end of the Second World War, at least eleven million people had been displaced from their home countries, with about seven million in Allied-occupied Germany. Two years after the war's end, some 850,000 people still lived in these camps across Europe.

Irina and her family's camp was not bad compared to what they had been living in during the war. It was an old German Army barracks, and at least it had beds. While Irina was there, she took nursing courses to become a nurse's aide. One day they needed a volunteer to work on a ship, and Irina volunteered. She was assigned to USS General S.D. Sturgis, a transport ship for the U.S. Navy which made twenty-one voyages between Germany and the U.S. and delivered refugees to Australia, Argentina, Canada, Brazil, and Venezuela. Irina went to Argentina and Australia, caring for mothers with newborn babies and young children. She worked on the Sturgis for nearly a year and a half.

One small comfort Irina experienced was on the trips back to Germany after they returned the refugees to Australia and Argentina. There were no passengers on the way back, just the crew, and so they would put on some "nice records" and listen to music as they sailed back.

The rest of Irina's family stayed in the camp to look for their father. They didn't know what had happened to him since he was stripped from them by the Russian army and sent to

Siberia. It was 1946, and they had not seen him in seven years. They wrote to the displaced person's bulletin board system in England that helped reconnect families of the war. Someone at the service saw their inquiry and notified Irina's father.

No one knows how Irina's father, Wladyslaw, got to England. When he was found and notified of his family's search for him, he was working in the kitchen supporting Anders' Army. Anders' army was a sizeable contingent of Polish civilians living in England who had been deported to the U.S.S.R. from Soviet-occupied Poland and brought together under General Wladyslaw Anders. Anders was a general in the Polish Army and, later in life, a politician and prominent member of the Polish government-in-exile in London. Irina's father was finally allowed to rejoin his family in 1946.

Irina's father was finally reunited with his family in a camp in Watenstedt, Germany. Irina was still working as a nurse's aide when she got the news that her father arrived. With their family now together, they were told they needed to begin the process of emigrating.

"I think it was around Christmas. I remember I was in Genoa (Italy) with the ship. We were getting passengers, and I received a letter from my mother that they had found our father. Once we got to Bremerhaven (Germany), I was able to take a few days off and see him. You know, he wasn't the same as the father I remembered. He used to rescue storks when they got between wires, and he was very nice to me—to all of us. And then, after so many years, he looked like a different person. I guess I was thirteen when he left, and then when I saw him again, I was grown up and working, and for him, I most likely looked different, too."

Irina didn't want to go to any place other than the United States, so she began applying. She had to find a sponsor who had a job and a place for her to stay in order to be eligible to immigrate. In 1949, she came to the U.S. Irina moved to New Jersey, where she stayed with a family and worked as a maid. Irina worked for a year while applying to sponsor her sister and brother. She got a small apartment and a job at a zipper factory, where she ended up working for twenty-nine years.

Her siblings finally came, but her mother and father did not. U.S. Immigration denied Irina's father's entry because he was diagnosed with tuberculosis. He had had an accident while in Siberia: a large log fell on his chest. Whether or not he had tuberculosis or a chest injury from the accident is not certain, but the United States government would not allow him into the country. Irina's mother stayed with her father in the displaced person's camp until he died there. She came to the United States shortly afterward.

Irina recently passed away. Her story is a reminder of one of the worst chapters in the world's history. Her survival and perseverance will always be remembered.

CHAPTER 4: GARY'S GRANDMA – PART 1

SHE LOVED THE HELL OUT OF ME

*G*ary lived in the projects. He shared a tiny one-bedroom apartment with his grandparents. While his grandparents slept in the bedroom, Gary slept in the other room that encompassed the living room, dining room, and kitchen. The small family didn't have a car until Gary was about 14 years old. However, they didn't need one. The grocery store and the bank were about a block away, and the Goodwill store was just around the corner. All they needed was a borrowed shopping cart from time to time. As a kid, Gary loved being pushed to the store by the person he loved and cherished the most: his grandma.

"Grandma" was her name. Everyone called her "Grandma": Gary's friends, wrestling coaches, football coaches, teachers, and neighbors. Even though Grandma stood at about 5'4" against

Gary's 400+ pounds and 6-foot frame, it was Gary who stood in her shadow. It was she, bespectacled, in her various assortment of colorful muumuus, who was the giant in Gary's life. She loved him more than anything, and she only wanted one thing in life for Gary: high school graduation.

"You know I love the hell out of you, but the one thing you're going to do is you're going to listen to me, and you're going to graduate from school." That's what she would tell Gary every time she gave him an ass-whipping. She would say to him that she loved him and demanded that he not go "gangster." He was going to graduate if it killed her. It was plain and simple. Nothing else mattered.

Grandma grew up during the Great Depression in Pennsylvania and had to drop out of the second grade to take care of her family. She never went back to school.

Gary rarely saw Grandma dressed in anything other than a muumuu with a belt draped around her neck. The belt was for the whippings. It was the instrument she used to make sure that Gary got through life in the projects without going to jail. She used the belt a lot on Gary. She made sure Gary had discipline from these whippings. Everyone in the projects knew about the belt, including his teachers and coaches. Corporal punishment was the way discipline was served, and back in the 1970s, it was not seen as abuse. It was just seen as love, tough love. She didn't want him to get into trouble, although it seemed that he found trouble everywhere he went. The whippings were the corrective action for Gary's habit of crossing the line into mischief. The belt and the whippings were the tools that were going to get Gary an education. School was so important to Grandma that she broke down and cried when he graduated from elementary school to middle school, middle school to high school, high school to college, and college to a bachelor's degree.

Gary's first encounter with tough love came when he was just 4 years old. Grandma was very protective of Gary. Some even thought she spoiled and indulged him too much, especially Gary's mother. Maybe it had to do with the fact that Gary's narcissistic, hustler mother had simply left Gary with his grandmother to raise, and Grandma felt sorry for him. Gary was very special to her. By the time Gary was 4, he still couldn't walk. No one could understand it. They took him to the doctor to have him checked. He had a high instep, but that shouldn't have prevented him from walking, jumping, and playing. Gary's inability to walk was a point of contention between Grandma and his mother. They would constantly fight about it.

"That kid can walk. He is playing you, mom."

"You leave that boy alone. He has an instep problem with his feet."

And so it went like this for some time. One day, on one of his mother's rare visits, Gary was standing up in his crib. He was holding on to the rail, jumping up and down, and having a great time. His mother just happened to pass by the room when he was playing. She immediately stopped, and her eyes locked with Gary. He stopped jumping, and he dropped right down to his bottom.

"I caught you," she yelled. "Mom, mom, I just saw that little bastard jumping in his crib! I knew that boy could walk!"

Grandma rushed to the crib, picked up a crying Gary, kissed him, consoled him, and told her daughter to leave him alone. Another argument ensued.

Several weeks passed, and Gary's mom came back for another visit. Still seeing Gary crawling around the tiny apartment, she hatched a plan.

Gary loved to be pulled around the neighborhood in a little red wagon. His grandma pulled him around every day. She was going to use that wagon to prove her mother wrong.

"Mom, I am going to take Gary around the neighborhood in the wagon," she said.

"Don't you dare pick on him! Don't give him any shit," Grandma retorted.

"I am just going to go for a little stroll and be with my son."

Gary's mom put him in the wagon and walked him just far enough out of sight of their apartment and the hovering eyes of

Grandma. She stopped. "You little bastard. I know you can walk. I am going to leave you right here, and you will have to walk to get back home."

Gary cried, "No, mama! Don't leave me!"

"I am leaving, and if you want to get home, you will walk!"

She left him there, sitting in the wagon. He cried as she turned the corner of the building and disappeared out of his sight.

Gary's mom rushed to get Grandma.

"Mom, come outside and watch this. I want you to see that Gary can walk."

They both went outside and peeked around the corner and saw a crying Gary sitting in the wagon.

After about 5 minutes, Gary stopped crying. He composed himself as best he could. Gary looked all around him and saw that there was no one in sight. The coast was clear. He threw his legs over the edge of the wagon, stood up, got the wagon handle, and started walking back home.

Incensed, Grandma came around the corner with fire in her eyes. They locked eyes, and Gary immediately fell to his butt.

"You lied to me! You can walk, and you had me worry all about it."

She proceeded to swat his butt. Gary's mom was standing in the background with quiet satisfaction written all over her face.

That was Gary's first encounter with Grandma's discipline.

When Gary was 9 years old, he had an insatiable interest in smoking cigarettes. All of his friends in the 5th grade were doing it, and he wanted to be just like everyone else. But, Gary needed practice. One day he stole his grandma's cigarettes out of her purse. It seemed like forever before she left the house! He was anxious to get going on his new habit but didn't want her to discover the missing pack before she left. When she finally left for the store, Gary sprang into action—he was finally going to be able to practice! Alas, he forgot the second thing he needed to steal from his grandma's purse to smoke: a lighter! With no match or lighter to be found in the tiny apartment, he decided to turn up the gas stove and light the cigarette from the flame—chalk one up to innovative thinking. Nothing was going to stop him! Gary lit the cigarette and began to pull drags from it. It was awkward, but thoughts of being "cool" floated around his head like the smoke rising off the tip of the cigarette. That was until grandma just happened to come back in the middle of his second drag. She had sensed that Gary was up to something. Up to no good. He was just too courteous, too interested in when she was going, where she was going, and how long she would be gone. It didn't take a rocket scientist to figure out he was planning something. With the oven burner still on, cigarette smoke wafting throughout the one-room apartment,

Grandma walked through the door. As Gary turned toward the oncoming footsteps, a "cherry" from his cigarette dropped onto the old plastic linoleum floor beneath Gary's feet. He quickly put his foot over the new hole it was creating. Grandma looked right at Gary with fire in her eyes.

"I knew there was something wrong! You stole my cigarettes, you little fucker, didn't you?"

"Grandma, I'm sorry, I'm sorry," Gary said, looking for any place to run. There was nowhere to run. Grandma picked up one of the Hot Wheels tracks lying about the house and commenced whipping Gary with it. He had "Hot Wheels" imprinted on his legs for days afterward. He never knew that she could strike him so hard that it could leave the logo on his skin.

Gary never stole from his grandmother again, nor did he ever smoke cigarettes.

When Gary was in the 7th grade, the school offered several mini-courses that students needed parental approval to attend. Courses like Sex Ed and Child Abuse Awareness were two such courses that were offered. Gary's grandmother felt it was up to the school to teach kids these types of subjects because there was no way she would have the birds and the bees talk with him. Grandma couldn't care less about what was being taught in school as long as Gary graduated. She signed the permission slip.

The teacher sat at the front of the classroom, turned the lights off, and began the slide show entitled "Child Abuse Awareness."

"A lot of you get a spanking at home, but there is a difference between a spanking and abuse," the science teacher started. A slide came up and showed pictures of belts, branches, irons, rolling pins, tennis rackets, and skillets. Gary immediately thought about the Hot Wheels tracks. "If you have ever been hit with one of these, you may have been abused." Gary sat up in his chair and thought to himself, "There is not one thing on that slide that my grandma has not beaten me with!"

"I think it was diabolical because back then, every time I did something, I got an ass-whipping for it, plain and simple. That's what happened. You got ass-whippings in the projects. I mean, kids talked about it, and they would laugh at you. 'Oh, your daddy whipped your ass the other day,' or something like that. So, I'm like, well, when you do something wrong, you get your ass whipped! My grandmother whipped my ass if I didn't do the right thing. How was that abuse?"

Gary came home that day after sitting through the Child Abuse Awareness class and had a revelation. He had a smile on his face from the discovery that his grandma was abusing him. He didn't think that he finally had something over his grandma, and Gary wasn't thinking about telling the school or the authorities either. None of that crossed his mind. He wasn't going to get her into trouble. He was going to get to play football!

Yes, football. Gary's second love right behind his first, his grandma. He knew why she was doing what she was doing and didn't resent her for doing it, strangely enough. He understood that the beatings were how she showed that she loved him, that she was looking out for him and his best interests.

"I got an out. I can play football a little bit longer tonight," Gary said to himself. He played football with the neighborhood kids on the grass-patched dirt field across from his home every day after school. It was the best part of his day. He loved to play football! It was the fact that Gary got called in for dinner by his grandma around six-thirty that he loathed. All the other kids got to stay out and play late into the evening. He wanted to play late in the evening, too!

Six-thirty rolled around and Gary's grandma, like she did every night, yelled out, "Gary, dinnertime, come on!" The football game just stopped.

"Man, you better go. Your grandma's calling you," said one of his friends. It was kind of a joke with the older kids because they knew that he would get his ass whipped if he didn't go.

"No, man, come on, we're going to play today. It's all right. It's all right. I got this," Gary responded.

"What are you talking about, man? You're going to get your ass whipped if you don't go home," his friends said.

"No, man, it's cool, it's cool. My grandpa said it was cool." They started to play. She called again. Gary ignored her. He had leverage tonight!

"Man, you are going to get an ass-whipping from Hell," his friends chuckled at him.

After the fourth call from his grandma, he relented. "Okay, man, all right, all right, leave me alone, guys. I'm going in."

When Gary walked across the dirt field toward his home, he could see his grandma standing, waiting for him, full muumuu and all at the end of the park. He knew that he was getting an ass-whipping. She gave him that look, and she was mad.

His grandma had a tongue like Michael Jordan's when he was about to slam dunk a basketball. Grandma would bite her tongue backward when she was about to whip Gary's ass. As soon as that tongue went back, he knew it was coming.

"Where the fuck were you," she scowled.

"I was playing football Grandma," he replied nervously.

"I called you at least three, four times, you little son of a bitch! Your dinner is cold. Get in here!"

"I didn't hear you."

"You know you heard me. Everyone heard me. I yelled! Get your ass in here. I'm going to whip your ass right now."

"You know, you can't use that big belt to whip me, Grandma!"

"What?" she said, sounding flabbergasted.

"That's a form of abuse."

"What the hell are you talking about?"

"At school, that permission slip you signed taught us about abuse and all those things. You hit me with that belt, that's abuse, and if you hit me, the police can get involved or something like that."

"You little motherfucker," and she went over to the telephone, picked it up, and dialed 9-1-1.

The Operator answered.

"Give me the police department."

"Yes, ma'am?"

A policeman answered.

"My grandson just disobeyed me, and now he's talking back to me, and he says if I whip him, you're going to come and arrest me for abuse! Well, I'm going to tell you what. You come down and arrest me now because he is getting an ass-whipping."

She put the phone down and proceeded to whip Gary.

"Grandma! Grandma! Grandma, stop!"

The police never showed up. That teacher had lied!

The next day, Gary went to his science class. His grandmother had called up the school and spoken with the science teacher earlier that day and told him what had happened. When Gary walked into class, bruises and all, his science teacher just looked at him with a smile and said, "Gary, come here. You know I'm just paid to teach this. You disobey me in my household, you get an ass-whipping, too. Now go back to your seat," the teacher said with a slight grin.

Gary learned that you didn't fuck around with Grandma. If you did the wrong thing, then you deserved an ass-whipping.

Gary was a star football player and state wrestling champion at his high school. He was big, he was fast, and he was strong. Colleges from around the country came to scout his talents. As a two-time state wrestling champion, he had only lost twice. All of this success in athletics made him a big deal at school. All of his success went right to his head. He started skipping classes. He skipped so many classes that he was in jeopardy of being suspended from school. His wrestling coaches feared that he wouldn't be able to wrestle in the upcoming match if he was suspended from school for truancy. They talked with him about it but it hadn't changed Gary's "ditching" ways. The coaches and the principal got together to discuss the situation. There was only one way they could get him back on track and into the classroom: Grandma.

The next day Gary went to his first class, which was actually his third scheduled class that day. He sat at his desk with his back to the door talking with friends when suddenly, it got quiet. His friends stopped talking. Their eyes widened. A hand from a 5'4" woman wearing a muumuu grabbed the back of Gary's hair and pulled him right out of the chair and into the hallway. Grandma proceeded to whip Gary right there in the school.

Gary never skipped class again, he made his wrestling matches, and won the state championship. Despite his success in sports, Grandma had never come to one event. She didn't care much about sports and just wanted him to graduate. If sports helped him get to that goal, she was fine with it.

"The way it was in the projects, if you didn't discipline your kids, they would end up doing drugs, smoking crack, stealing or just getting into trouble. Trouble that could put you them jail or trouble that would kill them. Discipline was unconditional love."

According to Gary, there was a difference between "an ass whipping" and abuse. He never saw those whippings delivered by his grandmother as for anything other than stopping him from doing the bad things he was doing. She always made sure Gary was cared for, but she didn't do it with hugs or words of affection. She showed her love with the belt.

In the projects where they lived, the two-story buildings were all set in a box configuration, creating a courtyard in the center. The courtyard was concrete. Most of the residents would sit, smoke cigarettes, drink beer, and talk. What else was there to do? There were pretty sizeable patches of dirt in one courtyard that the residents had made into small gardens. Little patches of ground where they grew vegetables. Gary's grandma had one of them. No one in the neighborhood touched it. Everyone knew not to. They feared a whipping. But more importantly, no one touched Grandma's garden because she would share with the whole complex whenever she harvested her vegetables. If anyone needed something, she did her best to provide.

"Within the community, you might think because people were so poor, they would steal or attack each other. It just didn't happen. People were in the projects for the same reason as everyone else there. People were just trying to get along. That was all they were trying to do."

Gary's family was just trying to get along, too. Grandma hustled and grandpa, suffering from schizophrenia-related trauma he experienced serving in the U.S. Army in the Korean War, collected disability checks. It was never enough. They often didn't have enough money to pay for the electricity and frequently sat in the glow of candlelight. They ate tomato sandwiches, mayonnaise sandwiches, mayonnaise and cheese sandwiches, ketchup and mustard sandwiches—whatever they could scrape together. They would put baloney and cheese on tinfoil and melt it on the windowsill to have something hot. They survived.

Gary had one set of clothes for school. Grandma made sure that this one set was clean and ironed for the next day, every day.

Grandma would wash clothes on a washboard then hang them on a wire in the courtyard. If she couldn't hang them on a line, she would heat the iron on the gas stove and press them dry. If they did have electricity, Grandma would dry them with a blow dryer. She was too proud to allow him to go to school in dirty clothes. Never. She always made sure she took care of Gary.

Grandma knew a guy with a truck. He was going through hard times, too. His wife had left him, and he could not afford daycare for his three kids. Grandma worked at a dry cleaner and was a maid for a wealthy family. She was always trying to make money. She hustled as many jobs as she could. Grandma hatched a plan with the guy with the truck.

"You wouldn't believe the stuff that these people are throwing out down there," she explained, referring to the wealthy neighborhood where her employer lived. "When I was younger, my first husband and I had a little antique shop. I see some things out there in people's trash cans that we could pick up and resell. Why don't we start a business together? We will take little Gary with us, and you bring your sons, and we'll go to these places in your pickup truck. I'll point out the things worth money, and our Gary and your boys will load it up in the back. We'll have a yard sale every week, alright?"

Grandma set the plan in motion. They searched the neighborhood for treasures and resold the bounty. Believe it or not, once they started doing that, the lights didn't go off in the apartment anymore. The mustard sandwiches were a thing of the past.

They would sell out every week and then go out again to pick up more "inventory." If you knew what it was to be hungry, you stole or got creative.

One day, they hit the jackpot. Grandma came across a child's vanity table and chair on the curb at someone's home. It was in perfect condition and made of cherrywood. They actually couldn't believe anyone would throw it out! The small crew loaded it into the truck. Grandma knew right off the bat that what they had found was valuable. Grandma told them to handle it carefully. While it was an antique, it was in pristine shape.

Finding the vanity set was like striking gold. Most of the items the crew discovered and resold were used, broken, and beat up knick-knack household items like silverware, mini appliances, toys, and sports equipment that would sell for two to five dollars. In Gary's neighborhood, families used cinder blocks and boards for shelves and milk crates and plywood as tables. The thrown-out items had value in Gary's neighborhood. The vanity set was a big find. Grandma wasn't thinking about selling it at her yard sale for two to five dollars. This item was going to sell for much more than that.

Grandma never put a price tag on any of the items in their yard sale. She would look at the prospective buyer and decide right then how much she would ask. It was all calculated in her head. Sometimes she would say "a dollar," and they would buy it. Sometimes she would say "three dollars" for the same object, and they would buy it. No one knew her formula, but she could somehow read her customers and get the price she asked.

A black car drove by their yard sale the day they put the antique vanity out. It was one of those luxury town cars. It slowed down as it passed, turned around, and crept by again.

"See that guy right there? He wants something here," Grandma said.

The car parked, and a well-groomed man in a suit stepped out. This type of car and this type of man were never seen in this neighborhood. Ever. He looked at the table and feigned a look of disinterest. He was smooth. Or so he thought.

"You keep your mouth shut; I'm going to show you something," Grandma whispered to Gary. The man came up to Grandma.

"How much you want for that table?" he asked.

She looked at him intently. "Well, you know this is nice cherry-wood here. It's a little bit old, but it is in great shape," she responded. "What do you think you want to give me for it?" she countered.

"I'll give you $300 for it."

There had never been anything in Grandma's yard sale over $20. Grandma's heart was pumping because she knew that she could pay rent and electricity for the next two months. They might even have a little extra money for the first time in a very long while.

"Don't you think that's kind of low?" she responded.

"Do you know what it is?" he asked.

"I haven't seen cherrywood like that in any other furniture store in the last thirty years, and I used to own an antique store," she said. "Exactly what it is? I don't know, but it's an antique."

"Lady, what do you want for it? What do you think is the price?"

"I'm a reasonable woman. I'm not looking to get rich or anything. You just give me a fair offer."

"$800. Is it okay if I give you $800?"

Grandma never really knew what the table was. It was old. It was a shiny, cherrywood table. Possibly handmade? She had no clue. It could have been worth thousands. It could have been worth a dollar. She had no idea why it had been out with the trash that day. But Grandma, with a straight face, said, "All right. You got a deal." The man handed her eight $100 bills. It meant so much! When she came home and told grandpa what had happened, he came over and gave Grandma a big hug and a kiss. "I can put food in the fridge, and I can keep our lights on. And we're going to get us a case of beer tonight!"

When Gary's grandma passed away, it rocked him. His anchor was gone, and without her, he felt listless. It has taken Gary a lifetime to work through the grief. He may never get over the loss. He did graduate from college. His grandmother lived long enough to see Gary graduate high school and go on to college. She cried the day he moved his mortarboard's tassel from right to left. She had achieved everything she had hoped for.

CHAPTER 5: GARY'S GRANDMA – PART 2

HIGH SCHOOL BRAWL

*G*ary was a Colorado State high school wrestling champion. In high school, he had only lost two matches, and they were to the same guy. At 6'4" and 385 pounds, mothers took their kids off the mat so they wouldn't have to wrestle Gary. They were scared. Gary was not only about twice the size of his opponents, but he was also phenomenally fast, with a crazed, focused expression that signified his commitment to winning. His intensity and passion easily outweighed him. He crushed his opponents. With the varsity success came an Aurora Central High School letter jacket that he wore with pride. But it was this letter jacket that nearly got him killed.

Gary and his buddies were walking out of the McNichol's Sports arena in Denver, Colorado, after the 1983 State Basketball Finals between their school and their cross-town rivals,

Montebello. The arena was a sellout, with nearly twenty thousand fans gathering to watch the two best teams in the state. They were bitter rivals at everything—so much so that it often got violent when they met. With Aurora Central letter jackets on and wearing the additional badge of jubilation that comes with a ten-point win at the Basketball Championship, Gary's group excitedly walked out of the arena. A steel pole-like barrier separated the teams' parking lots. On one side was the parking lot where the families of Montebello players gathered and tailgated. On the other side was where Aurora Central students and families parked. Gary, not paying any attention as he walked outside with "his crew," quickly found himself on the wrong side of that barrier.

"Gary, what the hell are you doing over there, man?!" yelled his friends. "Get back over here!"

That's when Gary saw them. About eight students from Montebello, noticing Gary's letter jacket and upset over the loss, walked toward him and surrounded him like a pack of wolves surrounding prey. One of the "wolves" circled Gary while the rest closed in.

"Well fuck you, boy. You caught up in the wrong place now, huh," said the circling leader of the group.

"Something you learn in the hood, okay, even when you're young, is if someone is talking shit and they do nothing, they're scared. If someone talks shit and then they attack you, then you are in trouble. I knew that this guy was just talking shit for about a minute—he wasn't going to do anything. But when about seven other guys joined him and surrounded me, and he just walked around me, I was scared, but I knew I had a chance. I just needed one more person with me," Gary recalled.

He heard in the background one of his best friends, Bruce, yell, "Gary's in trouble!"

Gary saw Bruce running towards him. He jumped over the barrier to his friend, and Gary now had that "one person" on his side.

"Okay, let's do this," Gary said.

The main guy stood back, surprised that Gary wasn't backing down. The encounter wasn't a bench-clearing brawl, it was a car-clearing brawl, with students from both schools rushing toward the fight.

"There were like fifteen motherfuckers around me. This ain't going to be no fight like, I don't know, between Cherry Creek or something. It ain't going to be like that. We're Central. Central was the high school in the old district. We had a lot of rough guys going to Central, okay? I mean, everybody didn't graduate, alright? Let's just put it that way. So, I'm a little scared, and when I heard Bruce say, 'Gary's in trouble,' I knew my boys were coming to help me. And you got to think now, I am 385 pounds and a state wrestling champion. I don't even go to class, alright? I work out in the weight room every day, and the teachers and the coaches don't give a damn. I can take all these guys with a little help."

As Bruce jumped over the barrier, the main guy doing all the talking lunged toward Gary.

"I hit him, and Bruce came from behind—I'll never forget it—I thought I felt something. Bruce hits this guy, and it's on, and all of a sudden, everyone started jumping over to help. We had a band member even grab his tuba and start using it as a weapon! We kicked the shit out of Montebello in that parking lot. They all ran for their cars."

When Gary and his friends got back to his car, their adrenaline was pumping.

"Oh, your ass was a little bit scared at first, weren't you?" Bruce asked.

"Yeah, I was scared as shit! Bruce, I owe you, man," Gary responded.

"Gary, I'm going to tell you something. I don't think he got you, but I saw something in his hand. It looked like something silver."

"What?"

"Yeah, that's why I hit that guy behind you because I saw something. You might want to check yourself."

"We were already driving down the road. I'm checking my back, and I felt blood. I stuck my finger in the middle of my back, and I felt a cut. I realized I had been stabbed by one of those guys! Right near the spine."

Gary had been stabbed near his spinal cord, but it thankfully hadn't punctured it because he was so big.

"Oh, shit, I'm stabbed in the back!" Gary shouted.

"You know they don't do shit for that at the hospital. They can't even stitch you up. You're just wasting money. You just got to keep it clean and let it heal," Bruce said.

"Here's the difference between a good American kid from the suburbs and me coming home to grandma with a stab wound in the projects," Gary explained. "'Grandma, I just got in a fight with Montebello. I think I got stabbed in my back. There's blood!'

"'Oh, you son of a bitch!' That's what she would say! That's what would happen. I am debating whether to face her reaction, go to the hospital, or have my boys clean up the wound!"

As the shock of the fight began to wear off, Gary began to feel the wound in his back and had no other choice but to go to the emergency room. After he drove his other friends home, he and Bruce decided to pull over on the side of the road. They lifted the back of his shirt.

"Yeah, you need to go to the hospital," Bruce said.

There was blood everywhere.

Gary and Bruce drove directly to the emergency room. All that was on Gary's mind was how he would get checked out by a doctor and back home before his grandma found out.

"If it doesn't take long, I'm good," he said to himself.

He was more scared of his grandma and what she would do to him than what the bleeding hole in his back would do. He could just hear her. "You son of a bitch! I told you that nothing good happens after midnight. Now, look at you!" Gary always seemed to get into trouble after midnight, and it was four in the morning as they drove to the hospital.

Because Gary was under eighteen, hospital admissions had to notify a parent or a guardian. No way was Gary going to have anyone contact his grandmother.

"Admit me, please. Admit me to the room before my grandma gets here, please," he begged.

They eventually called Gary's grandma, and someone had to get her because the family had no other vehicle.

"Dude, nah, I ain't taking your car and going to get your grandma," Bruce said. "You know what's going to happen to me if I take the car to your grandma's alone. She is going to whip my ass!"

Bruce compromised and went to get his grandma for protection before picking up Gary's grandma.

"I think this is one of the firsts—I mean, there were a few times that she genuinely was worried about me, but that morning when she saw me in the hospital, she looked petrified. She didn't say a word."

"He has a stab wound near his spine, miss," the doctor said to his grandma.

"Grandma, it wasn't my fault," Gary pleaded.

She was scared and stood silently, wringing her hands. Gary stayed in the hospital for a week because his blood pressure skyrocketed. He had never had high blood pressure before; despite his size, he always received clean bills of health.

"I was big. I never had any high blood pressure, none of that, but the doctors said it was high because I had just gotten in a big gang fight and was stabbed in the back."

The following day, everyone in the city had heard about the fight. It made the front pages of newspapers and was the leading report on televised news shows. One headline read, "'Mammoth Gary, State Champion, Stabbed in High School Brawl Outside of McNichol's Arena."

After a few days in the hospital and seeing that he was going to recover, his grandmother finally remarked, "You bastard! I told you nothing good happens after midnight! Why do you keep finding trouble?"

Gary just closed his eyes and pretended he was asleep. The police never did anything. The other Aurora high school, Hinkley, saw an opportunity. Because of all the news around the stabbing, school district officials discovered that Gary should have been going to Hinkley instead of Central based on his home address. They got a wrestling champion and All-State nose tackle. Hinkley forced Gary to attend their school for a week, but he was a Central Trojan forever. He was not going to betray a school that jumped the barrier to defend him that night. Gary refused to play sports for Hinkley and, with the help of his grandmother, was able to return to Central. He finished his wrestling career with one hundred and twenty-eight pins and two losses. The University of Oklahoma awaited him.

CHAPTER 6: I COULDN'T WAIT TO GIVE THEM EVERYTHING I HAD

The Vietnam War ravaged Vivian's country. Her enemy was now her ruler. Her father was taken as a political prisoner and relocated to the other side of the country. With little food or money to sustain the family, Vivian was forced to leave all that she knew and loved, risking her life on a long and dangerous journey to give her family the chance of a better life in America.

"At that time, we didn't know what escaping Vietnam looked like. Everyone talked about America as heaven. That's why it mattered. Even with the possibility that you would die, you had to take the chance to go. You had to leave Vietnam so that maybe you could get a better life. Maybe I could make a better life to help my family. If I didn't take a chance, my family would stay in Vietnam forever."

The day after Vivian's family celebrated her sister's engagement, she and her younger brother made their escape from Vietnam. It was June of 1978. Vivian's sister's friend had a boat that could take two people. He wanted to take Vivian's sister, but she had just gotten engaged and wasn't going to leave the life she was about to build with her fiancé, so at their mother's insistence, Vivian and her brother took her sister's and her friend's place. Vivian was 18 years old, and her brother was just 16.

"Communism was taking over the country. Everything was harder. There were fewer jobs, and people from South Vietnam couldn't have the same jobs as people in the North. If you weren't originally a Communist, the authorities would watch every move. You were limited in what you could do and who you could talk to. Our family was struggling. Without my father being there to bring in money, my family of ten kids was going hungry. It was worse for my family because my father had been a general in the South Vietnamese army. There was no future for any of us. Leaving was the only option we had. With me and my bother leaving, from my mom's perspective, it was two fewer mouths to feed."

Vivian was chosen to go because she was the oldest girl in the family. Vivian's mother pressured her son to go, not only to take care of Vivian but also to avoid being enlisted into the army. She didn't want what had happened to their other brother to happen to him.

"I had an older brother. After the Americans left, the Viet Cong tried to enlist all boys into the army. My mom sent my younger brother to somebody else's house to hide. One day, he missed my mom, so at midnight, he came home. Army officials were waiting for him and caught him. They put him in the army and sent him to Cambodia. He drank the water there. The water had chemicals from all the bombs that had been dropped. He got sick, and they sent him home. Six months later, he passed away of cancer because of the chemicals in his body. He was only nineteen or twenty. He was young. And that's why my mom decided to send my other brother with me on this escape. I had four brothers. My other brother was in the 'secret' army—they put him in jail, too. We didn't see him for a couple of months. We thought he died. He escaped and came home in only his underwear! He had had to remove his uniform because if they saw him wearing Army clothes, they would have killed him. He needed to take off and hide, and that was why it took him a couple of months to get home. When he stood in our house, we didn't even recognize him."

Vivian's father had been in the army for fifty years, and on the day the Viet Cong took over, they imprisoned him.

"I remember we were at the Army base with my dad. Oh my God! We saw the guns and there was shooting all around us. We saw people around us die. We were hiding, my mom and all my sisters, while my dad was trying to help protect the base. There was no American support. They were gone. When the fighting was over, I remember seeing my dad just sitting and crying. He knew that the Viet Cong were going to come and get him soon. And we just sat there with him and waited for them to come and get him. They took my dad. Gone! I was so scared. We were so young to see the guns, the shooting, the bombs, all kinds of things no one should see. Oh my God! I couldn't even sleep at night! Too many bad memories."

It would be twelve years before Vivian would see her father again.

It was eight o'clock in the morning when the car came to Vivian's house. It was time to go. The first stop on their escape would be at a staging house of sorts. The house's location near the beach was a perfect place to quickly get to an awaiting boat off the shore. They had to have the ability to leave at a moment's notice.

"We had to sail at night when there was no moon. If the authorities caught us, they would put us in jail," Vivian recounted.

They made multiple attempts to leave each night, but they were thwarted by moonlight or patrolling police. Finally, one night around 2 a.m., under cover of a moonless night and with just the shirts on their backs, they were able to get to the shore without being noticed. The awaiting boat was about a hundred yards offshore, unable to get closer because of the dense seaweed that could tangle in the propellers.

"We saw the boat, but it was so far out that we needed to swim to get to it. And I didn't know how to swim! It was lucky that my brother knew how. We walked out as far as we could. I was so scared. My brother said, 'Vivian, wrap your arms around my neck. I will get us there. You must help me kick because if we are too slow, they will leave us.' I told him I was too afraid. 'If you walk back to shore, the police will get you.' I had no choice. I held on to my brother and kicked with all my might."

They reached the boat with several other people and headed for a nearby island to wait for a larger boat that would take them on the long journey to Hong Kong.

"We stayed on an island for a couple of days. It was miserable and freezing at night. We had no food, no water, no shelter, no nothing. One day we saw some people walking on the beach with guns. They came to rob people because they knew that many people escaping from Vietnam had money or gold. We fled deep into the island to hide. I remember being so scared. They never found us."

This experience wouldn't be the last time Vivian and her brother would face someone trying to rob them. Each time they transferred boats and were handed off to a new handler, they put themselves in danger of being robbed, abandoned, or killed.

"One time, when we were changing from one boat to another, the boat captain picking us up asked our captain why there weren't more people to take as had been promised. Our boat driver told him that one family had stayed back because they got sick. The other boat driver pulled a gun on all of us and told us that we had to pay the money they lost because the other family wasn't there. They wanted only gold. My brother and I had no gold. I only had a little bit of money sewn into my clothes in case we needed it. Finally, someone else on the boat paid the man in gold for us, and we were able to go on."

Fifty-two people were in a small boat that should have only been carrying a third as many people. Many became ill on the five-day journey to Hong Kong. At night, they were wet and cold. It was blistering hot during the day, and the constant rocking of the boat made everyone nauseous and irritable. Tensions were high. Not only were people cramped on the boat, seasick and hungry, but there was very little potable water, causing severe dehydration. Conditions were desperate.

"I didn't eat or drink anything for four or five days. There was fighting on the boat because everyone wanted water. There was very little water on board. I was so seasick that I couldn't keep anything down; I just threw up whatever I swallowed. My brother was so good and strong. He looked after me. I wouldn't have made it without him. He would walk the boat and find a little food and water and bring it to me. In my weakened state, I almost fell overboard because the boat was violently rocking. He tied me to the boat after that scare. He told me that I could throw up all I wanted to now!"

Fortunately, a larger Chinese fishing boat happened upon Vivian's listless vessel. They tethered the vessel and brought all the people on board. The Chinese family gave them food and water and told them that they would take everyone to a port near Hong Kong.

"If we hadn't seen them, I don't think we would have survived. The family fed all of us, and they gave us water. They even gave us some money, too. They took us close to Hong Kong because they didn't want us to get caught by the police or the Navy."

When Vivian and her brother got to the port near Hong Kong, they got into a smaller boat for the short sail into Hong Kong.

"The money and the food they gave us, we had to throw in the ocean. If we got caught with 'Hong Kong' money and food, they would think we were from Hong Kong and wouldn't let us into the refugee camp to get to the United States."

The Vietnam War had created a major Vietnamese refugee crisis in the 1970s. Tens of thousands of Vietnamese people, primarily from faltering South Vietnam, fled the country seeking asylum. Refugees lived in "open camps" while they waited for resettlement in other countries, primarily the United States.

Vivian's journey to the refugee camp in Hong Kong took over a month as they had traveled over 800 nautical miles from Vietnam.

Before Vivian and her brother could be admitted into the refugee camp, they had to be quarantined and processed. Hong Kong immigration authorities took them to a small island outside of Hong Kong, where they had temporary housing and a small medical facility for incoming refugees. For the first time in over a month, Vivian was able to take a bath and sleep in a bed.

"They had three different camps. If you were lucky, they put you in the camp inside the city. You weren't lucky if the authorities put you on the island. We were out on the island. We didn't have any money and didn't do anything for weeks. We just waited for the time when our names would be called to leave for America. The Chinese family with the fishing boat had liked us. Their son would come and visit us in the camp often. He gave my brother and me a little bit of money and would bring clothes and dry food."

After a while of being in the camp with no money and no prospects to make money, Vivian and her brother snuck out of the camp, took a boat, and went to Hong Kong. They wanted to be admitted to the "city camp." They hoped that from there, they could make some money while waiting for their approval to go to the United States.

"We had friends in the camp in the city. They let us live there with them. You had to have a pass if you wanted to leave the camp. We never had a pass. My brother and I climbed the fence to go to work every day."

It was nearly three months after leaving their family in Vietnam before Vivian could get word to them that they had made it to Hong Kong and were okay. Working through the Red Cross, Vivian sent a letter to her mother.

"Oh my God! My mom told me later that she almost passed out when she got word that we were okay. She was so happy, and all my sisters cried. My mom and family thought we were dead as they hadn't heard from us for so long. There were a lot of people who tried to escape but died or were kidnapped or enslaved. Pirates would catch refugees, rob them, kill them, and take the women to be slaves."

Vivian and her brother were in the refugee camp for nearly a year, waiting on their uncle's immigration sponsorship from the United States to be approved. Vivian didn't know that her uncle in America, her father's brother, was fighting to convince his wife to agree to the sponsorship.

"We waited and waited for a whole year. When we first got to the camp, the authorities told us that we could leave the next day if we wanted to go inland. Even if we didn't have any shoes, they would let us resettle in Hong Kong. But my dad wanted us to live with his brother in Colorado. We had no idea that my aunt was the reason why the sponsorship paperwork and the resettlement took a year."

Vivian's aunt saw no benefit in sponsoring them. Her uncle was a reluctant co-conspirator. She wasn't interested in supporting and being responsible for them. It wasn't until Vivian and her brother finally got to their aunt and uncle's home in the U.S. that she saw how much her aunt had developed a hatred for them.

"We finally got to my uncle's house. We lived there for only one month. They put us in a small room in the basement. It had two small beds. My aunt wouldn't let us eat at the same table with them. We were only given whatever was left on their table. We didn't need a lot, but it wasn't enough food. It was just scraps, leftovers. They ordered us to clean the house, cut the grass, groom their two dogs, and wash their car every day. It didn't matter if it was cold or hot, we had to do all kinds of things, but they would not feed us anything other than what they left on their table.

"My aunt worked during the day. While she was gone, we were so hungry that we found a sixty-nine-cent can of beans, opened it, and shared it. My aunt's mother was at home and saw us. She told her daughter what we had done. We were just so desperately hungry. At 2 a.m., she woke us up. 'Why did you guys take the food and eat like that?' she asked. I told her we were sorry, but we were so hungry! We needed something to eat! She told us that we could never take any food without asking her first! She yelled at us for taking a little can of food!

"Later, my aunt and uncle had a party, and she made me cook all kinds of food. I knew how to cook. I prepared the meal. When the party started, she locked us in the basement. She didn't want anyone to see or talk to us. I think she didn't want anyone to know that she was stealing the two hundred dollars my brother and I got for welfare. I didn't know that she took it, copied my signature, and cashed the checks. I kept waiting for money because I wanted to buy some food and send some money to help my mom back in Vietnam. We waited and waited until one day we went to the welfare office. Our English wasn't so good, but we did meet with a man that helped us. He told us, 'Yes, you received three checks, and they have already been cashed.' I said, 'Really? I never saw any check.'

"My aunt and uncle had put a lock on the mailbox. The only phone in the house was locked in their bedroom. We were prisoners. They didn't want us to have contact with anyone. When the mail came, they took it and opened it. Whenever a friend sent a letter, they would hide it. We had no friends. Nobody. No nothing. For a month, oh my God, it was as if we lived in hell. We slept with the dogs. They peed and pooped right where we slept. It was unbearable!"

During the day, Vivian and her brother were reluctantly allowed to go to a local church for English lessons. Vivian made a couple of friends there and told them what was going on at her aunt and uncle's house. The friends decided to go to the house and help Vivian and her brother leave, but her aunt wouldn't allow them.

"No, you cannot leave this house. I forbid it," she told them. The aunt was holding Vivian's and her brother's Social Security cards and their identification paperwork. She had locked every-thing away, preventing them from leaving. It wasn't until Vivian's friend went to the police that her aunt and uncle finally relented and let them go.

For months, Vivian and her brother went from house to house, staying for a week at a time. They did have the Vietnamese community that opened their homes to them, but that didn't mean it was cozy, safe, or comfortable. It often meant meager, confined, and the floor.

"We were in a terrible situation. I didn't know which was worse, Vietnam or America."

Vivian and her brother could never unpack their suitcases as they shuffled from house to house and passed from one stranger's home to the next. Their stays were cut short because of poor conditions or being robbed of what little they had by their hosts.

The church began to raise money to help Vivian and her brother find a place they could rent. Vivian was now 20 years old, and her brother was 18. They found an apartment in Boulder, Colorado. Rent was two hundred dollars a month. While they didn't have anything like blankets, cups, or utensils, they finally had a place for themselves. Vivian and her brother stayed there for ten years. They slept on the floor and covered themselves with newspapers. One day, while they walked to the English language school, a car passed with a twin-sized mattress tied to the roof. Vivian and her brother ran after the car. They asked the driver if they were getting rid of the mattress and if they could take it. Vivian and her brother now had something to lay on. It was old and it was dirty, but at least it wasn't the floor.

For the next ten years, Vivian and her brother went to language school and worked. Vivian found a job in Boulder making men's ties, where she worked for ten years. They paid her by how many ties she could make. The more ties she made, the more money she made. Her brother worked seven days a week, ten hours a day, in a small metal-works factory. They used the money they earned to buy food and some essential items for the apartment and sent some back to Vietnam.

Back in Vietnam, Vivian's family was struggling. Her father had been taken in 1975 by the Northern Vietnamese Army and put in a prison camp, tortured, and forced into hard labor. The rest of the family had little means by which they could survive. Vivian and her brother had to make it to freedom to build a life and help support the family back home.

Vivian met her future husband at a friend's birthday party. They dated for a year and then got married in a small ceremony at the local church. They worked hard to buy a home so they could sponsor her family.

She was pregnant with her first child when she went to the airport to pick up her parents. It had been twelve years since she had last seen them.

"God! I couldn't believe it! I saw my mom and my dad. We were all crying. I couldn't wait to give them everything I had."

They all lived together for another five years. Vivian worked hard and took care of everyone. Vivian, her husband, and their three kids stayed in the master bedroom. Her mom and dad lived in one room, her two brothers in another, and her four sisters remained in the basement. They were together again, ready for a new life in America.

CHAPTER 7: I'VE ALWAYS HAD A CONNECTION WITH DEAD PEOPLE

*S*he always wanted to be a coroner or a mortician. Dealing with dead people attracted her; she felt like she had a connection with them. She wasn't frightened or scared. Ironically, her name was Angel.

Ever since she was a little girl, she could see them. She could see dead people, although, at the time, she had no idea they were dead. She could see them as plain as the nose on her face. The problem was that no one else could.

Her two best friends were Charlie and Emily. She played with them every day. They would run around in the park, play dolls in her bedroom, and have tea parties together. They were genuinely real people to her. Angel never thought of them as ghosts or anything like that. Her interaction with them concerned her mother that she took Angel to a hospital to have her tested. The doctors never found anything wrong with her. Her mom was petrified of what she was doing and seeing and always told her that she had to stop!

Stop what? They were her friends. The little boy and the little girl were her best friends. They weren't "imaginary," as her mother constantly claimed! They were as real as anything in her life. They were friendly, and they were never threatening.

"They never harmed me," Angel recounted. "We just played and talked together."

However, that was about to change…

"One day, when I was 6 years old, I was in our backyard and decided to swing on our swing set. The swing faced the back of our house. I jumped onto the seat and began to go back and forth until I felt a firm push behind me. I thought it was my mom, but no one was there when I looked back behind me. When I looked toward the house, I saw that my mom was in the kitchen window washing dishes. Another push sent me swinging forward, and it startled me. I swung back and was then forcibly pushed forward again! I yelled for my mom! She didn't come. She just continued to have her head down at the sink washing dishes."

Angel didn't know what to do. She frantically clung to the chains as she was forcefully thrown forward. She looked at her mom in the window and yelled again, "Mom! Help!" But when she saw her mom in the kitchen window, she saw that Charlie was standing behind her with his hands on her ears, holding her head down toward the sink.

"She couldn't hear me! She couldn't see me! I yelled again, but nothing changed. Charlie was still holding my mom's head firmly down with his hands over her ears! So, I jumped off the swing and landed very hard on my right leg. I screamed in pain, but my mom didn't respond. I crawled to the back door and began to bang on it, yelling for my mom. My mom finally came running to the door."

"Angel, what happened?" her mother asked.

"Mom, I hurt my leg," Angel said with a grimace, in agony.

"Why didn't you call for me, Angel?"

"Mom, I did. I don't think you could hear or see me because when I called for you, I saw Charlie standing behind you with his hands on your ears, holding your head down to the sink."

Her mother was exasperated. "Angel, you have to stop this! If you tell me one more time about this Charlie and Emily, there will be no birthday for you and no Christmas presents! You have to stop with this game!"

From that day onward, Angel no longer saw Charlie or Emily. Not having a birthday or getting any Christmas presents was motivation enough for a six-year-old to turn something off.

When Angel was older and going to school to be a coroner, she looked up the house she lived in on the Internet. She found something astonishing. Apparently, in the 1920s, a young mother had killed her two children in the house Angel grew up in. Their names were...

CHAPTER 8: IT WAS MY BEST DAY

*B*arry couldn't help but think to himself what a small world it was as he sat in the car with his blind date. Eileen had been married to one of Barry's fraternity brothers back at the University of Buffalo. That was close to twenty years ago.

"I asked her what her name was. She told me, 'Eileen Mann.' I asked her where she had gone to school. She said, 'Buffalo State.' Bells went off in my head. Eileen. Buffalo State. In college, my roommate's good friend was this kid named Jeff Mann who was going out with a girl, who became the Fraternity sweetheart, named Eileen Terry. I am like, 'oh, shit.' What a small world. I hated that guy like you could not imagine. The only reason I let him get into the fraternity was that he was friends with my roommate. He was the biggest jerk in the whole world. He was such a big braggart. She was divorced from him when I met her because he was so bad. He actually went to prison.

"We had an excellent time on the date. Eileen was an interior decorator at the time. I invited her over to my house for dinner and asked her if she would design the upstairs of my house because I had never finished it. She did all the design stuff for the place, and we started to date."

After Eileen finished the design, they decided to move in together and find a place in Manhattan. They had the money to buy into a co-op. In a co-op in New York, the building itself is considered a corporation. Every apartment "owner" is a shareholder in the corporation. As with any corporation, the co-op is run by an elected board of directors. The committee made all the decisions regarding who would be accepted or denied ownership.

"Co-ops weren't very big on single people, and they were very prejudicial about who they hired and who they let in the building. At the time, there were no restrictions on them, no guidelines, no laws, and no rules. If they didn't like Blacks, Jews, whomever, they would not allow them to buy in. If they didn't like what kind of job you had, they wouldn't let you in. If you had too many kids, they would deny you. They would reject you for almost any reason, regardless of the legality. It was whatever suited them and their beliefs. We were rejected from one building because I owned a collection agency. They didn't like people that owned collection agencies, believe it or not. It was that kind of thing. So, for the next co-op we approached, we changed the wording of my business from 'collection agency' to 'insurance recovery.' Many of the co-ops we approached were also concerned because I had four kids, and she had two kids. They didn't want a building with a bunch of kids. We had to put in that we only had two kids that lived with us, which was true, and we got in."

Six months after they met, Barry and Eileen secretly married in a courthouse in New York City.

"The reason we got married was that we wanted to apply for a co-op in Manhattan. We did it secretly. None of our friends or family knew. It was February of 1984. I had been seeing her for about six months. It just felt right. You know this was 'the one' kind of thing. It was not a rebound thing like the last time I was married."

Barry and Eileen would later have a ceremony before friends and family the following June. It was Barry's third marriage.

"My second wife wanted a break while she reorganized her life. I was taking care of our child before I met Eileen. She had two children, 10 and 13."

Barry and Eileen lived on 77th street in Manhattan until Barry's collection business began to get into financial trouble. They had to sell the apartment.

"We got divorced so that it would be easier financially, and they wouldn't come after her for anything. We had been married for about twenty years. I had to start over. We each got our own place, but we saw each other every day. It was more of a convenience divorce. She had assets that we didn't want to be tied together. Bankruptcy was a bitch. I would never wish it on anybody. Our friends and families still knew we were together. It wasn't like we were apart. We'd see all the grandchildren together. We were just living in different places. Our children were starting to have kids of their own, so we were always together with the grandchildren. We also had two dogs. We shared them. I had the dogs on the weekends, and she had them during the week. Her parents hated me because they felt like I put her in a bad position with the divorce and the bankruptcy. Her parents were nasty people. Everybody knew how nasty they were. Her mother was the meanest person I have ever met in my life. Even their grandchildren, Eileen's kids, couldn't stand her. They wouldn't even let me go to her apartment because they bought her the apartment and didn't want me there. I had to pick up the dogs in the hallway! It was like that until after she got sick, and then they had no choice. They weren't going to take care of her."

Eileen was diagnosed with Parkinson's disease.

"She kept saying to me that there was something wrong with her leg. She couldn't move her leg. It kept dragging. She was young, about 59. Eventually, she began to get the different symptoms that came with Parkinson's: twitching and head bobbing that drove her nuts. She was extremely vain and, being a real estate broker, she needed to look a certain way, especially in Manhattan with these high-level people. I used to go with her in the car and take her to a showing because Eileen couldn't know if she would have an episode. Eventually, she had to stop working. It got to be too much. I had to get someone in the house to take care of her. Once she stopped working, she went downhill pretty fast because she didn't have that outside interaction to keep her mind going. She had a hard time being by herself and was always in a panic. She couldn't be alone anymore. She was incapable of taking care of herself. She would fall and hurt herself and she started to get dementia. I was still living in my apartment. I used to go over to her place every other night and sleep there just to help her to feel safe. She was always afraid. We eventually decided that I had to move in, so I gave up my apartment and moved back to take care of her. She said that she didn't trust anyone else. I was there for eight years until she passed away. I didn't sleep in the same room with her because I snored, and she would not have gotten any sleep. So I slept on the couch in the living room for eight years.

"It was a struggle. It was tough. I couldn't go anywhere even though I had full-time help for her. She was despondent when I wasn't there. She depended on me so much that she couldn't do anything by herself. She couldn't shower or dress or do anything. It was hard. Really, really hard. It was probably the worst thing I had to live through. I had been through tough times, but nothing was worse than this. Watching someone you care for slowly lose everything is tough. It was a debilitating disease because she didn't know what was happening to her.

"I made sure that I took her out every weekend—to lunch, to dinner... just to get her out. Otherwise, she would have just vegetated away in her apartment. During that time, I helped her visit her grandchildren and see them grow up. She enjoyed that. She relished that a lot. She lived long enough to see her grand-kids in their teenage years, fortunately."

The family always celebrated the Thanksgiving the weekend before the holiday. This gathering would be their last Thanks-giving together.

"It was on a Saturday. She seemed fine. We had Thanksgiving dinner at one of her daughter's places. We spent the evening with our entire family. When we came home, I asked her, "How did you feel about going out to see the kids?" She said, "*It was my best day.*" Those were the last words she ever said to me. When I woke up the following day and went to her, she was stone cold. It was extremely frightening. It was tough finding her that way. I had never met death like that in my life. It was my first experience seeing death face to face. I tried to revive her, but she was just so cold. There was no chance.

"Jewish people bury their loved ones right away. It was within a day or two that we buried her. It was amazing how many people showed up. I was shocked. The combined families, the exes, everybody was there. It was like a whole scene from a movie. My daughter decided to have a wake instead of sitting shiva. When sitting shiva, friends and family come in and talk about the person's past. It is pretty quiet and solemn. My daughter decided it wasn't going to be that way. She was going to make it more like a celebration of her mother's life. You couldn't imagine the amount of food that was there. There were so many people in the apartment that they were wall to wall. There were 250 to 300 people in that apartment. It was crazy. Everyone liked it, and it was fun. It was nice. It was a beautiful event. I am glad she did it."

What waited for Barry after going through all of it would also prove to be complicated. Eileen's family wanted all of her possessions and eventually kicked Barry out of the apartment where he had cared so intently for his ailing ex-wife.

"Her parents hated me from the very beginning, and they hated everybody who any of their kids were with. It wasn't like I was unique. They were control freaks—especially her mother. Her mother was a lunatic and was the sickest, cruelest person in the world. She would even accuse her very young great-grandchildren of stealing from her house when they came to visit! She was just a crazy person. Everything was about money and control. She would give them money for college but with strings attached. Eileen broke away from them when we got married, but when we got divorced, she needed their help, so that became the 'strings' again. It was very tough to deal with the situation. They let her know that they would help her get a new apartment, but it would be in her father's name only, and I was not allowed to step foot inside. We were still together, and they knew it, but they kept me out of the apartment. That was one of their rules."

Eileen's name was not on anything, even though she used her money to buy the apartment. Her parents wanted to protect her from any creditors, and she was not in a healthy condition to manage her affairs. As the threat of any creditors diminished with Barry's financial improvement, they had tried to put the property back in Eileen's name. However, the co-op wouldn't allow the transfer because she was a real estate broker and didn't have a steady income.

"When Eileen died, everything was left to her sister. Eileen loved her sister, but her sister was full of shit—greedy like her mother. I said to her sister, 'Give the apartment money to the kids when you sell it. I will stay there until then because you will get more money for it.' She wouldn't give it to them, and she kicked me out for suggesting it. She kept all the money for herself. The kids got nothing."

Barry moved out, taking little with him but memories. Still working 10+ hours a day, he devotes his time to his adult children and grandkids. He often sits in his beautiful apartment overlooking the East River in New York City, reflecting on his life, family, and Eileen's ability to find joy in life's blessings.

CHAPTER 9: DIANA'S SECRET

*W*hen Diana felt the nodules under her left arm, she thought they would just go away, so she delayed a doctor's visit. When the swelling remained and she could wait no longer, her physician gave her what would ordinarily be devastating news: the nodules were a symptom of stage 4 stomach cancer. They offered her a couple of treatment options, but she didn't give them one thought.

"Being a nurse, I had taken care of people who had all different types of cancer. My father died of colon cancer. I always said if I got cancer, I was not taking any of that treatment because I saw how devastating it was for some people."

Before giving Diana the diagnosis, the doctor asked if Diana would like him to call her family to come to the hospital.

"I was in the office by myself. I said, 'No, just tell me.' He told me I had six months."

The cancer had spread all over her body. Her prognosis was grim, but Diana walked out of the hospital calmly and with her head held high.

"My husband picked me up. I told him that they said I had cancer, and he started crying. I wasn't crying, but he was crying. I said I wasn't going to take any treatment. He said, 'Oh, you're going to,' and he convinced me. So, for his sake, I decided I'd take chemotherapy."

Diana didn't want anyone else to know she had cancer. She would go to the hospital, get her chemo treatment, leave, and try to be as normal as she could be. Her husband asked her if they should have a family meeting.

"I didn't want to tell anyone anything about this if I didn't have to. So, I didn't tell anyone anything. The way I lived my life, I thought I could probably get away with the secret for a while if the chemo didn't devastate my looks and things like that. I didn't want to hear all those voices from my family. Some would probably have been very opinionated, and I didn't need to hear that, and I didn't want others to worry. So, I never told my children. I didn't tell my mother. I didn't want to deal with people knowing. I didn't want to get the 'sorry' phone calls. I didn't want to be bothered about it. I just felt it was my cross to bear, and I would bear it with dignity. I made the right decision,

I believe. To this day, I don't think I needed whatever they were going to offer me. I just knew that with God and me, I would be okay. Whatever the doctors thought they could do, I would just accept it. I just thought to myself that this was my time. Cancer was the way I was going to die—exit this stage. I accepted it."

Diana went to her regular chemo appointments for three months, taking everything in stride and keeping the treatments, the pain, the sickness, and the worry all to herself. She was committed to living life as normal as she could. Her doctor was amazed at how well she was doing.

"I talk about you in all of our staff meetings because you're doing so well," he told her.

Diana's health steadily improved, and her six-month death sentence soon passed. She stopped the intravenous chemo treatments and switched to pills to continue her journey to recovery.

"After about two years, I decided that the pills worked well but that they had done all they could do. I wasn't going to keep taking them anymore. I was feeling fine, and the pills were turning my hands really dark. I didn't want to walk around like that and really could not understand why I still had to take them. I called the doctor's office to tell him I wouldn't be taking those pills anymore. I no longer needed them. That is when they told me that the doctor that had originally diagnosed me had died! I outlived my doctor!"

The doctors checked Diana out and agreed that she was in remission and could stop taking the medication. She was cancer-free! She could get on with life as she had been living but without the burden of the illness and the secret.

Five years after her initial diagnosis, Diana decided to tell her secret to her family, but she wasn't going to do it in the privacy of her own home. She had other ideas to let everyone know what she had gone through.

"I was at church, and we have what they call a Testimony Service, where you have something big to report. I decided that I would tell everyone there my secret."

Diana's family, sitting as part of the congregation that day, were shocked as they listened to Diana. Her brother began to cry upon hearing the news. Her mother just looked at her in disbelief. Friends and family were utterly stunned. They had no idea that she had had any illness, let alone a six-month cancer death sentence. Her husband was telling everyone around, "She took chemo, and she didn't even lose her hair!" Her husband had never realized the truth of what Diana had gone through. She had been determined to keep her secret. She wore a wig that was so natural that he had never discovered the truth.

It has been nearly a decade since Diana was given just six months to live.

"We're all terminal, and even when the doctors say certain things, it's doesn't necessarily mean their prognosis is always accurate. My body responded in a way they had never seen before. All I know is I'm still here, and I'm doing quite well despite it. I only share this when it's necessary because I never want anybody to feel sorry for me. That's not how I live my life. I live my life as a contributor and an asset to myself and others, and feeling sorry is not my thing. I'm still here, and I am glad about it. I am a survivor."

CHAPTER 10: ONE NIGHT IN CHARLOTTE

*J*erry and his friend Peter walked out of one of the best concerts they had ever seen. The Wide Spread Panic show had delivered as promised, and their third-row-from-the-stage floor seats put them in a spot where they felt that they were a part of the show. Jerry's cross-country trip from Seattle to Charlotte, North Carolina to see his favorite band with his best buddy, had been worth it. Caught up in the echoes of the music dancing around in their memories and laughing about the 'girl' who flashed her bare chest to Michael Houser, the Panic lead guitarist, and seeing Houser's reaction, they made for the exit. Jerry was grateful that he had not missed the concert by almost missing his flight out the day before.

When they reached Jerry's car, Jerry felt for his cell phone. It wasn't in his right front pocket like it always was. He frantically patted all about his body, checking all the pockets in his pants, his coat, and his hoodie. Nothing. A rush of anxiety ran through him. It was gone.

"I freaked out. Through all the adrenaline of literally the best show I had ever been to, I thought I must have dropped it somewhere! I looked at Pete and freaked. Like everyone, my whole life was on that damn phone."

Jerry and Pete quickly retraced their steps back to the arena, looking frantically for it. It was dark, and they were pushing against the wave of exiting concert-goers which made it even more challenging to hunt for the phone. Their search led them back to the arena door they had exited. The phone must have dropped out of Jerry's pocket in the arena!

"The security guard told me to 'beat it' and that there was no way we were getting back in the building. He told me the best I could do was to go to the Lost and Found at the arena box office the next morning!"

Pete had a brilliant idea. He would call Jerry's phone! They would be able to get together with whoever answered. Problem solved.

"We just weren't thinking clearly at the time. We were running all over that parking lot, going against the crowd, and arguing with the security guard. Finding that phone was going to be like finding a needle in a haystack. We could have eased my anxiety quite a bit by calling it when I first realized I had lost it. Funny when you lose your mind in relative hysteria. I couldn't believe it took us so long to figure that out!"

Pete dialed Jerry's number from his phone. He heard several rings. After the fourth or fifth ring, he was beginning to think that no one had found it, and he imagined it on the floor under a seat, laying in beer and popcorn and probably broken. Pete looked at Jerry and shook his head. There was no answer. Then, serendipitously, Pete's eyes lit up when he heard someone answer, 'Hello.'

Maddie and her friend Julia were also out of towners from Pittsburgh who had come to see the Panic show. Like Pete and Jerry, they too saw the woman flash her breasts to the band.

"All of a sudden, this girl steps up onto her chair and practically takes her shirt off! I never expected that at a Panic show! It was a crazy show, and I will never forget that," Maddie said, recounting the scene.

When the show was over, and the house lights came on, Maddie and her friend hung out and just took it all in. They sat down in their seats, sweaty and exhausted. They had been dancing for the past two hours.

"Jules and I were just sitting down after the show, waiting for the clean-up crew and security to kick us out, when I saw a light flash on the floor. It was a phone! Someone had dropped it. I went over and answered."

Jerry had dropped his phone. Maddie had picked it up. That simple little event was the beginning of a life-long love affair.

When Jerry and Pete met up with Maddie and Julia at the arena exit, Jerry and Maddie had no idea what was about to happen. It was an instant attraction.

"I just saw this girl, and I couldn't take my eyes off her. When she greeted me, she had this huge smile. I had no choice but to give her a big smile back. It was weird because when we were smiling at each other, Pete and Julia just didn't exist. It was instantaneous. That had never happened to me before. I completely forgot about my phone, to be honest."

The feeling was mutual. With the phone in her hand, Maddie saw Jerry and her heart skipped.

"I remember handing him the phone, and I just felt butterflies."

The four concert-goers decided to find a nearby diner to get a bite to eat. Jerry was immediately thankful that Maddie had found his phone, and Maddie was grateful that Jerry had lost it in the first place. The four sat for hours talking about the show, where they were from, and how funny it was that they had all come from out of town to see Panic when they serendipitously stumbled into each other's lives. They shared much in common, including a mutual love for hiking and the outdoors. It was like a dream until they were shaken awake by the admission that they each had significant others. That realization bummed them both out. Before this meeting, they had both been happy in their long-term relationships, and neither was looking for anyone else. They were both just out having fun in a strange town, now with strangers.

After they ate and talked well into the night, Jerry and Maddie exchanged phone numbers, friended each other on Facebook, and promised to stay in touch. With many 'chance' encounters, the promise to keep in touch doesn't last very long, but for Jerry and Maddie, it did. They kept in contact even though they lived 2,500 miles away apart. Through IMs, Instagram posts, Facebook updates, and phone calls, they shared information about their families, jobs, significant others, and lives. They maintained a meaningful long-distance friendship for three years.

When Jerry quit his job, he called Maddie to share how mistreated he had felt. When Maddie broke up with her boyfriend of four years, it was Jerry who she called. He was the shoulder that she would lean on, putting a relationship that had been such a big part of her life behind her. Jerry's relationship with his girlfriend was steady and comfortable but lacked those intense feelings that seemed to have been lent to Maddie the day they met. It wasn't that he wasn't happy with his girlfriend—it was just 'ordinary.'

"I loved my girlfriend. She was a great person. We had a lot in common and had been going out for two years or so. I guess that I just kept searching for the feeling I had when I met Maddie that night."

When Jerry broke up with his girlfriend, Maddie was the shoulder Jerry leaned on. Maddie felt sorry for Jerry. He was a good guy, and she hated seeing him heartbroken. They talked long into the night, both realizing how close they had become despite the miles between them. Spontaneously, they decided to see each other in person and picked a spot on the map that was halfway between them. They considered Minneapolis, but it was winter, and Minneapolis wasn't doing any relationship any favors with below-freezing weather. They contemplated Kansas City. It just didn't seem 'interesting' enough. Denver. They both loved the mountains, and they loved to ski. It was decided. The Mile High City it was!

When Jerry and Maddie saw each other in person for the first time in three years, it was like they had never been apart. The intense feeling that struck them that night in Charlotte was burning even hotter. They were friends falling in love. They spent the three-day weekend together, picking up where their long-distance conversations left off. They laughed, they skied, they made love, and they departed at the airport with a mutual, "I love you."

"That weekend in Denver changed my life. I had never been more into someone. I had never felt such feelings," Maddie recalled. "It was just one of those moments where you tried to stop time. I think we both knew we only had three days, and we grabbed on to each minute."

The physical distance between Jerry and Maddie would not stay for long. Within a month, they quit their jobs, told their families what they were going to do, and moved to Denver.

"My parents thought I was completely irrational. Over the years, they had heard me talk about this girl from Pittsburgh but had never met her. They couldn't understand that I was dropping everything and moving to another state for some girl. I just had to do it."

When they got to Denver, they were cautious. They each rented separate one-bedroom apartments in the city but were so close to each other that they essentially shared the same bed each night. After six months, they ditched their places and moved in together. After another six months, they were married. Seven years later, and with a 3-year-old son, they are a happy family still amazed at that night in Charlotte.

"I completely believe in fate. How else could something like what happened to Maddie and me have happened? I cannot believe it to this day. What blows my mind is that I almost missed my flight to Charlotte. If that plane hadn't been delayed, I would have never made it there."

CHAPTER 11: HE BROKE EVERYTHING IN ME

*M*eg was never known for making impulsive decisions, but her friends and family thought she was making a big mistake this time. What she was doing was entirely out of character.

"Everybody was terrified because I wasn't the person that got into real committed relationships. I didn't make rash decisions. My friends thought this was not at all like me. They all thought I was being brainwashed. He put me on a pedestal. I think that that was what some of that appeal was. He had that edge. I was such a wholesome girl, but I also have always liked that edge. Small town, big dreams."

Brad.

Meg cannot explain why she made such a quick decision to marry Brad, but her upbringing may have had something to do

with it. Meg had grown up in Dwight, a small town in north-
east Illinois. With approximately 4,000 people, it was a tight-
knit, provincial community where everyone knew each other.
Living in such a rural, remote, and protective place didn't offer
the chance to meet many people outside of her community. She
grew up fast when, as a teenager, she had to assume the responsibility of caring for her mother.

"My mom had stage 4 breast cancer when I was 13, and then she
relapsed when I was 18. With my mom being so sick, I focused
on life and death rather than adolescent stressors such as what
you wear to school or what boys you like. I missed a lot of that.
There was a solid year where she was in and out of treatment. I
think the toughest part was watching her go through it all. It
just messed with all of us mentally. Her condition was always in
the back of our minds. I think that's why I essentially missed out
on my adolescence.

"Growing up in such a small town, I had known all of my male
peers since I was a toddler. I saw them eating glue and crayons!
There weren't a lot of dating options in Dwight. I didn't want to
end up living, marrying, and raising kids in Dwight. I just
wanted to get out and move on. So I went to college, and that
was the first time I really dated. I wasn't serious with anybody
there, though. I did have a boyfriend for two years, but I was
never really into him. It was kind of like, 'Oh, maybe we'll get
married, maybe not. I don't care.' My boyfriend was safe and
comforting, but there were things about him I didn't like. He

was from a small town like me. He grew up in a small farm town outside of St. Louis. He wanted to move back there, and I didn't want that. I think that's where we were just so different. Other guys at my college were interested in dating me even when I had this boyfriend. There were guys I had crushes on and liked, but no one that would make me flip who I was like Brad did."

After getting her degree in Physical Education from Quincy University, a small, private, Roman Catholic, liberal arts school in Quincy, Illinois, Meg moved to St. Louis.

"I had a lot of friends from St. Louis, and my college boyfriend was there too. As soon as I got to St. Louis, though, I met Brad and broke up with my boyfriend."

Brad.

"He was a manager at a Bally Total Fitness Club in St. Louis, and I came in as one of his personal trainers. I liked him. There was just this chemistry with him—something I had never felt before. It just knocked me off my feet. It was almost like out of a movie. I was so attracted to him and just liked the things he said. I liked the way he acted. As soon as I met him, I thought he was what I wanted and the person I saw myself marrying. We got married within four months. We met at the beginning of June, he proposed to me in August, and we were married by October. It was just boom, boom, boom. He knew what I wanted and presented himself in exactly that way."

Meg and Brad's relationship developed quickly. He knew how to act and knew what to say. Meg was ready for a man to fall in love with.

"When we were first together, he would quote verses from the Bible, and he came across as being such a religious, Godly man. I had a lot of spiritual beliefs that had helped me to deal with my mom's health struggles, and he played off that. I think that was what scared me most about all of it. He took a shot at my Achilles heel. He just came and swooped me off my feet. He had me move in with him right away; he took care of me financially and emotionally. He was so doting and loving. But that honeymoon only lasted for so long. His true colors started to come out. There were red flags from the beginning, but I think I missed them because I was so in love, so swept off my feet by him. I think I was immature, but I didn't know that at the time. I think I just didn't realize that I needed to be careful because you can get swept up in a controlling, bad relationship if you don't know the warning signs."

Meg's friends and family expressed concerns, but she had blinders on. Everyone around her was worried about the relationship.

"My friends were going to my parents and asking, 'Why is she marrying him and what is she doing? What's happening? Is he brainwashing her?' Many family members were concerned—so many people, and I just couldn't see it. I loved him.

Meg quickly realized that Brad had a temper, but she initially dismissed his actions since the anger was directed at objects; she overlooked the telltale signs of controlling and coercive behavior.

"For instance, he got mad at me one time and punched a hole in our bathroom door. It started with stuff like that. He took a milk carton and chucked it across the room; it exploded against the wall. There were warning signs."

Brad wanted to control Meg's every move.

"He had me move in with him after a month. I was young and in a new, big city. It was the first actual metropolitan area I had lived in. It felt safe to have someone like that. So I think I wasn't picking up on the red flags. When Brad was my manager at Bally's, he changed my work schedule because he didn't want me working nights anymore, and he only wanted me to work at certain times. He was controlling from the very beginning, and I didn't even see it. Once we got married, that's when things shifted. He went from this loving, adoring, put-me-on-a-pedestal guy to... 'I was like the shit on his shoes' person. There were so many messed-up layers, and I think there was mental illness there. There was a history of it in his family. He was constantly bouncing from job to job. It's so weird to me now that I could fall so far down a rabbit hole with someone.

"He had real control issues. He would misquote Bible verses to match his agenda, saying, 'A man's in charge and a woman is to be submissive.' That was how he started controlling me, and it got progressively worse.

"I remember one time he told me that my family wasn't my family anymore... that he was my family. We were driving to my parent's home which was four hours away and we were fighting. We were fighting all the time. He took my credit cards and threw them out the window, and when we got to the house, he said, 'That's not your family! I'm your family!' He messed me up with the games he would play. He would hit my dog for no reason. He would go after the dog because he knew that the dog was my dog. He was just abusive."

By all accounts, Brad was manic and impulsive, and demonstrated sociopathic behavior. He had grown up in a dysfunctional family. As Meg began to learn about how his dad had died of alcoholism and how abusive he had been to Brad's mother, Meg started to see—but not fully acknowledge—the warning signs in Brad's actions. The dysfunction of his family was taking on a life of its own in their relationship.

"The worst thing that I remember was him pushing me down in the bed, putting his hand over my mouth and telling me to shut up. That was the scariest he ever got, and then he left me, which was the most shocking part of all. I'm not sure if it was him being impulsive or me just being really clueless, but I was shocked. I had no clue."

After all the verbal abuse, the controlling behaviors, and the physical altercations, Meg was still committed to the relationship even though she had expressed her unhappiness and considered divorce several times. She felt that she had to persevere. She was raised in a Catholic family and was committed to her relationships.

"I would tell him I wanted a divorce and that I didn't want to be with him as I walked out the door, then I would just go back. I thank God that he left. I think his leaving was by God's grace. I do. I don't think I would have ever decided to leave him because I had such firm religious beliefs. Right before he left me, we had this terrible blow-up. He pushed me and I flew backward, and then he slammed the door in my face. It was four o'clock in the morning. I got in the car, and I drove home to my parents in Dwight. I spent the weekend asking myself, "Do I want this to work?' I still remember to this day thinking, 'Yes. I want to give this my all. I don't want to have any regrets. I want to make this work.' I also had a firm religious belief that you don't get divorced. I was raised Catholic, and that was a part of it. You stayed married 'till death do us part.' There was that Catholic guilt in me. I didn't want to be lettered as 'that woman who is divorced.' It's a real thing. I returned to him, and I remember saying, 'I've had time to think, and I don't want to be divorced. I want to make this work.' And he said to me, 'I do want to be divorced, and I'm leaving you.' I was like, 'He has to be kidding. This has to be a nightmare—it can't be real.'"

"That was just a sucker punch. I know it's crazy, but I don't think I would have left him. Maybe if he had put me in the hospital—I hope I would have left him at that point. I don't know. Maybe that was just God's way of telling me, 'I am going to kick the door open for you because I don't think a controlling personality like his decides to leave on his own accord.' It never happened in the stories of abuse that I've read! Brad deciding to leave was a blessing because it could have turned out really, really bad."

After a year and a half, the marriage was over, but the relationship was not.

"He broke me spiritually, emotionally, mentally, and physically. He broke everything in me. But even more messed up was that during the divorce, he still tried to manipulate me. He told me that the way I handled myself with the divorce would determine if we got back together or not. And I fed into it. I hired a mediator instead of a lawyer and got completely screwed in the divorce. No money, nothing. He sold and profited from the house we had together. He still had control over me."

The control continued well after their marriage ended.

"We had a break where we didn't see each other for eight months after the divorce, but then we got back together for another year."

Meg's friends were in disbelief that she would resume her relationship with Brad after all she had gone through in her marriage.

"One friend couldn't talk to me anymore. She had to quit talking to me. I get it. It hurt so much, and these were the friends that were with me through it all. My one friend bailed me out by giving me five thousand dollars to pay off credit card debt, and I thanked her by going back to the abuser who put me in debt? I would be fucking pissed too. 'I paid off a credit card that your shitty husband gave you, and you're back seeing him again?' My friends were upset, and I don't think those friendships will ever be fully repaired. That's probably my biggest regret. It sucks that I destroyed friendships because of the bad decisions I was making."

Meg continued to see Brad until she moved out to Colorado. They stayed in contact even after the move. Brad would come and visit, and they were in touch regularly through text and phone. There was an opportunity to move back to St. Louis when Meg was offered a "personal training dream job." It meant management and money—a job and position she always had aimed for.

"There was this bizarre spiritual moment I had. I was driving toward Boulder looking at those foothills, and I finally decided that this was not healthy. I remember saying in my head, 'Meg if you go back, you're going to end up marrying this bipolar man again. You're going to have crazy bipolar children. You will never move on. You won't like your life. It will never be better. You will just keep swirling in an unhealthy relationship.' That was the first moment that I realized I had to let go—after a year in Colorado. It was time. This guy was not changing. He had multiple relationships in St. Louis while keeping me at the ready to use at his discretion. I had been in denial for so long, that was the first time I realized that he would never be the guy I needed him to be. I cut all ties with him. I changed my phone number. I called my parents to cancel the plans to move back to St. Louis. We had already booked everything. My dad was about to fly out to Boulder to escort me home when I called and told my family I couldn't move back. I needed to stay in Boulder. Of course, my parents were like, 'Great! We will cancel the U-Haul and still send your dad out, and you guys can just have some father-daughter bonding time.' And that's what we did. My parents were relieved that I was cutting ties with Brad. Finding my home and independence in Boulder was the first step of me moving forward."

Once Meg had decided to cut ties with Brad and move on, she took her time getting healthy and rebuilding her life.

"I didn't want to keep falling into the same pattern of another bad relationship, another bad marriage, another bad divorce, and being treated like shit at every stage. That's why I didn't get married or jump into another serious relationship right away. I knew I wanted something different, and I couldn't jump right back in. I needed to heal because I wasn't healthy. A lot of times, when you're in such toxicity, you just keep gravitating towards toxicity. You keep repeating the same cycle, and you can't get out of it. You're not even aware that you are gravitating towards the same thing until you step back from it and see that this is messed up. All I had known for so long was dysfunction. I didn't even know how to be healthy."

Meg spent eight years treating the scars Brad left her with and reflecting on the causes and effects of her poor decision-making. Spending those years in self-reflection helped her recognize the ingredients of a healthy relationship before meeting Mike.

"With Mike, there was stability. We took it slow. I wasn't going to allow myself to get in that toxic situation again. I didn't want my judgment clouded again. There was something with Mike. He was just so patient with me, and I even told him I had some trust issues that would take me some time to overcome. I think just meeting Mike—so solid and secure and just so kind—helped me move on from these scars."

Now married with two children, Meg reflects on the lessons of that terrible time and the value it has brought to her present-day life.

"I don't feel that I'd be in this place if I hadn't gone through that experience. I think battling the intensity of that situation brought me a lot of strength. I wouldn't change it. I gained a lot. I don't know if I could have appreciated Mike the way I do if I had not had this horrible relationship first. I hate saying that, but I know who I was back then. I took it for granted and assumed that every relationship was good and that everyone was treated nicely. I don't think I had a terrible, negative experience until that marriage, and it took time to heal and learn and mature.

"It made me a better person, and it made me stronger because I've been through some tough things. I think that some of what I went through had to do with how young I was. I was only 22. I did think at the time that I was marrying a good, wholesome man who would provide for me and love me unconditionally. I thought I had realized the dream until those layers started coming off, it was like, 'This guy is messed up.' Brad broke everything in me—the scars may remain, but I have healed, and I'm stronger than ever."

CHAPTER 12: NO ONE'S GOING TO BE HAPPY FOR ME IF I'M NOT HAPPY FOR MYSELF

*T*he day Natalie's half-sister was born was the day that changed her life forever. As her mother was giving birth that day, Natalie was having her arm broken by her stepfather. Her 'stepfather' became her 'sister's father' at that moment. Natalie was 3 years old, and that day began a life at home that was filled with terror, abuse, and struggle for survival.

"My mother told me that was the night that everything changed because that was the night that I wouldn't sit in the back of the car. My mom had been in labor for eight hours at the hospital when she gave birth to my sister. I'd been at the hospital waiting with my stepdad all day. I was exhausted and cranky. He took me out to the car and wanted to put me in the car seat while he got the stroller out of the trunk. I wouldn't sit in the car seat. I was fussy and having some sort of fit. He got very irritated with me and grabbed my arm to put it through the strap, and he pulled too hard and ended up breaking my arm."

"My mom said that my stepdad and I had a great relationship until the day my sister was born. I almost felt like my family disowned me that day. It was never the same. I never got that 'dad' figure from him that I can ever remember. He just wanted everything to go right for his daughter, but not for me."

Alcohol would play a significant role in Natalie's life. She recognized early on that her stepdad had a problem.

"My stepdad has always been an abusive drunk. He would go to extremes to punish me, like pushing me down the stairs, or if I was 10 minutes late getting home from the school bus, I was essentially going to get my ass kicked. It wasn't just the things that would be used to discipline a child. It was things that would put me in the hospital. I was in the hospital a lot, and I had my fair share of stitches. I have lots of scars from his abuse. I have a big scar on my arm that I got stitches for when he put me in a dog kennel. He put me there a lot. I have a scar right below my eye from the time he pushed me down the stairs. There were times where he would spank me but to the point of blistering. Even when I was older, like 16 years old, he was still bending me over his fucking leg to blister my ass. 'No one's going to love you when you got black eyes. You're ugly now,' he would tell me after he punched me in the face. I had a lot of concussions. He would grab me by the shirt, swing me around, and he didn't care if my head hit the wall. I can remember a time when he locked me out on the back deck in the backyard. It was one story up from the ground. He had been doing work on it and hadn't put the railing up yet. I started screaming because I was like, 'How the hell am I supposed to do anything out here?' I was trapped. He finally let me in, and when he shut the door, my finger got caught in the door, and I had to get stitches on my finger because the tip of my finger was just missing."

The abuse was so bad that Natalie sought help from her school, teachers, and the police. Still, everyone disregarded her complaints as just another rebellious kid, and her mother would reinforce that perception by adamantly telling them all that her daughter was lying. She couldn't get help from anywhere, and while she admits to being a challenging teenager, her story shows a clear cause and effect. Her acting out was a plea for help. It was the only way she knew how to communicate her situation to the people and authorities around her.

"The school system didn't care. I never got good grades, so they labeled me a 'bad' kid. What upsets me the most was that these teachers were out there, and they spent a lot of their time with us as kids, and I was always acting out! I needed help! They never recognized what I was going through. They just thought I was this tough kid. They called my mom every day, and none of those teachers thought to ask if things were going okay at home because I was acting out so much.

"I had lunch detention almost every day. When I was in middle school, I told one of my teachers, 'I'm getting beat up at home!' I would go to school with bruises and cuts that everyone could see. One time, I had a hand mark on my arm from my stepdad grabbing me and throwing me down the stairs. My teacher saw it, and he got Child Protective Services involved. I begged them to take me from that house because I didn't want to go back home. When I had meetings at my school every week with CPS, I would tell them what was going on. The sad thing is that it is fully legal in Colorado to beat the shit out of your kid as long as they have a roof over their head and food in their belly. 'You can do whatever you want to your kid' was what they told me every time. They couldn't do anything. And this wasn't the 1950s; this is happening now. I would call the cops and beg them to take me because I didn't want to go back home, and they never took me. They never did. I purposely got in trouble so that the cops would be acquainted with me and my situation. They knew who I was, but it didn't matter. I ended up getting a breaking and entering charge when I was 14. I got suspended from school for three months. They put me in a place where you spend the night with a bunch of other girls, sleep in bunk beds, and go to school. It was like juvie, but not exactly. When that program was over, I begged them to not make me go back. I would tell them that I was just going to keep getting into trouble so I could come back. They would just say, 'We'll see you soon.' I was so scared to go home because I didn't know what kind of mood he was going to be in."

When the police responded to Natalie's calls, her mother and sister's dad would maintain a unified front.

"I'm getting the shit kicked out of me and would call the cops. When the cops came, my mom would make up a whole new story and tell them that everything I said was a lie. I was just so mad. Even when the neighbors would call the police about what was going on in our house, I wanted to tell them everything, but my mom would threaten, 'If you tell them what really happened, you'll be in real trouble.' My mom was so manipulative. She would tell me, 'You know, you're my only friend.' Because of those words, I would keep doing this fucked up shit that she made me do, like lying to the police about what was happening. She knew it was wrong, but my mom, honestly, is crazy. She is with this man for money, and she had been saying for years that we was going to die because he's a horrible alcoholic. She's put me through this abusive relationship growing up just because she swore he was going to die, and he never did. And in fact, he's still here to this day, which is just nuts to me."

"When I was 16, I ended up dating this guy. He had a criminal background. He was 18. He didn't tell me about his criminal background, and I didn't know that everything he was telling me was just a lie. I introduced him to my family. My parents didn't get a very good vibe from him, which I understand now. They researched him, and he came up on a registry for exploiting a minor and sexual assault. I didn't believe them. So, I would sneak out every night and meet up with this guy because my parents wouldn't let me see him during the day. One night, I got caught. When I went out, I didn't know my parents were following me. Suddenly, a car pulled up and my sister, her dad, and my mom got out of the car. They were screaming for me because they thought I was in danger. They knew that he was a predator and thought I was in trouble. My sister's dad and I got into a huge fight at the park. He ended up punching me in the side of the face. Neighbors were looking out the window. One of the neighbors saw him slug me in the face and ran out of his house in his bare feet and his boxers, tackled him and beat him up. He told him, 'Don't ever fucking touch a woman again,' and called the cops. Even when the cops came, I begged them to take me that night. They still wouldn't take me. I finally had witnesses, and they still didn't take me! I felt lost, honestly, because even after that, there was nothing I could do. I was stuck no matter what I did. At that point, I just gave up."

Throughout Natalie's childhood, the abuse continued. She took things day by day and frequently ran away from home, spending nights anywhere she could.

"I spent a lot of nights at parties or in a park. There was a sewer drain, and I would go in there and sleep. It was lonely, but I couldn't go home. I couldn't go to my friends because I was too embarrassed. What could they do for me when the police couldn't do anything for me?"

Natalie's mother was not just a bystander to the abuse. She was not just an enabler to an abusive husband. She also contributed to the continual breakdown of Natalie's relationship with her sister's dad in a very self-serving way: her cheating.

"Growing up, my mom always had three or four boyfriends while married to my sister's dad. I can rattle 16 names off the top of my head of men she had an affair with. I knew what was going on, but I was never allowed to say anything. Since I didn't have a very good relationship with him anyway, I never said anything to him. My mom would make me start shit with him so we could leave. She'd tell me to throw pencils or whatever at him so he would come to beat my ass so that my mom could say, 'That's it! We're leaving.' We would go to one guy's house, and we'd have dinner. We'd go to another guy's house, and we'd have dessert, and then we'd go to another guy's house and spend the night."

Natalie's mom also forced her to shoplift.

"My mom was a brain surgeon, and she had money, but if I needed anything, my mom would always just tell me to go to the store with a backpack and fill it full of things I needed. Little did I know, my mom was doing the same thing! We would go to the grocery store, and she would make me ride in one of the handicap scooters, and she would put all the stuff she was going to steal under the seat and tell me, 'No one is going to give you shit if you're a handicapped kid.' She had an eBay store and would sell all this stolen stuff on eBay. One day, she ended up getting caught. We were walking out of the grocery store, and my mom had bought a gallon of milk but had two to three hundred dollars' worth of stuff in her purse. Security yelled at her, and she tried to run, leaving me behind with all the stuff she stole. Fortunately, she was tackled in the entryway. She ended up getting this huge fine for stealing, and I ended up going into foster care. I was in the system for a year when I was 16."

Shortly after coming back to the family from foster care, Natalie's stepfather made a plan to remove Natalie from the family for good.

"My mom went on a trip to Washington for work. My sister's dad took me to court, where I had to sign these papers to get emancipated from the family because he didn't want me in the house anymore. He took my phone away so I couldn't call anybody to try to stop this. I was just clueless and didn't know what to do. I was 17 years old and didn't have any life skills. I was still in high school. When my mom came back from Washington, I wasn't there."

Natalie had been forcibly emancipated and kicked out of her house before her mother returned. Her mother had signed the papers before she left on her business trip. She left the action to be taken by her husband while she was away. Natalie was now on her own.

"When I moved out, it was very tough because I had no place to go. I had no credit to get an apartment. I was living out of my car for a couple of weeks before finding a place that would take me. I was sleeping in my church parking lot. I went to school and washed my face in the sink because I didn't have a shower. I played softball. My mom and dad never went to any of my softball games, but my sister played too, and they were huge supporters. We had a shower in the locker room, and when I was done playing softball, I would take showers because I just had to go right back to my fucking car. I had to pay a security deposit and first and last month's rent upfront to get an apartment. It was a lot of money. I think one month's rent was $1,250. It was very tough, and it took me a long time to save money. I was working at Good Times Hamburgers, and as soon as I had saved enough, I moved into that place, but I couldn't tell you how many times I went hungry. I would call my mom for $5, and she'd just tell me, 'That sucks.' It was tough, and money was very tight, but I made it work."

Natalie had to drop out of school so that she could make enough money to live. She eventually got her GED.

Through it all, Natalie's relationship with her sister wasn't good either. Although they grew up in the same house, they had completely different and separate experiences.

"I was very envious of my stepsister growing up. We didn't have a very good relationship because her dad would go to the extent of covering up what he did to me by saying, 'That's discipline,' every time he beat me up. He brainwashed her so bad that she started to believe it. He was putting me in the hospital, and she would just be like, 'Well, you shouldn't have done that.' She didn't have to get the beatings that I did. She was accepting of the fact that I was just being punished and deserved it. He used me as an example to her."

Natalie has a twin brother. When Natalie's parents divorced, they split custody of the two siblings between them. Natalie's dad took her brother and gave up his rights to her. He didn't want a daughter. Natalie went with her mother. Natalie's brother is currently in prison for murder, but she has built a relationship with him over the years.

"We have a very healthy relationship, and we're very close, but he is going to be in prison for a while."

Today, Natalie is on her own. She has gone through a lot since being kicked out of her home. Her relationship with her family, including her mother, doesn't exist.

"I don't have a relationship with my mom at all. She is a cheating, lying, thieving fucking bitch. She's insane. I don't have a good relationship with anyone in my family."

Since being on her own, Natalie has taken steps to build her life and find security, friends, and love, but it hasn't been without challenges.

"I made a resolution. I just decided to cut my family out of my life. I didn't want to deal with the stress from it anymore. I went and grabbed everything that they had of mine—I took it all. I even asked my grandmother to take down all the pictures she has of me. I don't even have a very good relationship with my grandparents because I have told them the shit that my mother, their daughter, has done to me, and they think I'm making it all up. They see my mom as this perfect person who hasn't done anything wrong and that she's this amazing doctor, blah, blah. I got tired of hearing that I was out here fucking up and not taking lessons from my mom. I don't have a relationship with them for that reason."

The decision to cut ties from the family has come at a high personal cost and great personal courage. Being on her own and having to reconcile her stepfather's abuse and her mother's shoplifting and philandering has posed significant emotional challenges.

"I was doing a lot of drugs. I got very involved with heroin and Percocet. I felt like I needed something to kind of ease the pain. It took a lot for me to come out of that spot. I still go to AA for drug abuse. I needed an escape, and I felt like that was my only option. As far as anyone could see, we were just a nice suburban family, but it was what happened in that house that fed my habit."

"I finally stopped after I got in a terrible car accident. I had just shot up and wanted to go to Lookout Mountain because I was having a bad night, and it was snowing. I hit a very old lady and her granddaughter, and they had to go to the hospital. I said to myself, 'I'm going to fucking kill someone if I don't stop.' I found a cool support group on Facebook for people that would talk about how they got over their addictions. I started reading stories about people and how they would get hurt or how it affected their family, and I was like 'I have to stop.'"

At 21, Natalie has been through a lot and reached her lowest point a year ago.

"I spent Christmas by myself two years ago. In January of last year, I was actually on suicide watch. I didn't want to be here anymore. My family planned a secret trip without me and didn't include me. It was a reality check that I had no family. So, I tried to take my own life. I was actually on life support just a year ago. It's definitely because of my family, but now I have made it. That was when I made my resolution to take the toxicity out of my life."

Having made that big decision, Natalie looks to the future with hope, happiness, and love.

"I am going to school to be a veterinarian, and I'm working at a vet office in Boulder. I'm very happy right now. I moved my boyfriend out here from Nebraska. I live in a 2-bedroom apartment on my own, and I can do it. I think that's an accomplishment. It's exciting because I know many of my friends can't say that they have their apartment. I think that's a good thing for me. Despite everything, I can do it. Working to pay rent every month is an accomplishment. It's so stressful, but then once I finally pay it, that feels like an accomplishment. That's what I've had to tell myself because I just never got that support from my family. No one is going to be happy for me if I am not happy for myself.

"I've also discovered a lot of things about myself. I love to paint, draw, and write. That's exciting to me. I'm pretty happy where I am right now. I am very passionate about what I like. I love dogs. They are so therapeutic. I feel like my job is therapeutic, too, in a sense. I get to go and play with and care for animals. That's exciting for me."

CHAPTER 13: I'M NEVER GOING TO BE YOUR WIFE

*A*gi was working as a nanny in New York City. As she entered the building where the family she worked for lived, Laszlo, the building's doorman, opened the door. They were both having the time of their lives in a place far from their respective homes. It was 1993, and at the time, they never imagined that this brief encounter would lead to a life-long love affair, marriage, and two children.

How did Laszlo arrive at this spot in front of this building at this time to meet his future wife? His journey started in 1987 over 4,000 miles away in Kaposvar, Hungary. He was 18 years old and a Mitsubishi Starion teased of possibilities beyond his country's borders.

Kaposvar is located in the southwestern part of Hungary, 70 miles from the Croatian border.

"Through my girlfriend, I met a Hungarian couple who had just come back from Australia. They brought with them this nice car. I thought to myself, 'If they could do it, I could do it, too.'"

Laszlo had never seen a car like it on any of the streets in his town. The Starion was a two-door, turbocharged four-cylinder hatchback sports car. It was beautiful. It was fast. It was from the West.

"I rode in this car as we were going from club to club one night. I had never been in anything like it. I thought to myself, 'This is what it is like in the West.'"

Laszlo decided shortly after that to apply for a visa for Austria.

"My mom found out from her friend who worked at the police station that I had applied for and got an Austrian visa. When my mom came home, she raised hell. She asked me what I was doing, where and when I was going, and how I could do this without telling her. She looked all over the apartment for the visa I had hidden. She couldn't find it. I had hidden it under the rug she was standing on while she was yelling at me. She gave up and told me to leave the house keys in the mailbox if I left. The next day, she and my father left for work, and I left the keys in the mailbox."

"Fortunately, I got the visa before being drafted to the army. It was mandatory service for all 18-year-old boys. It was part of the reason I left. I didn't want to serve for two years. I wanted to travel and see the world."

When his parents came home and found the keys in the mailbox, they called the border guard at the Hungarian-Austrian border. With just $500 in his pocket and a backpack, their only child had left for the West. It was too late—he had already passed through the border checkpoint. He had successfully hitchhiked the entire 200-mile journey between his home and Vienna.

"By the evening, I was in Vienna. An Austrian guy had picked me up and had taken me to his house and fed me. I took a shower, changed my clothes, and we went to the club! I thought this was 'great!' He bought me some hashish, and we smoked it all night! When we were done, he asked me where I wanted to go. I told him I wanted to go to Germany. So he dropped me at the highway to Germany and went home. I had a sleeping bag with me and found a place to sleep that night in the park around Schönbrunn Palace."

Schönbrunn Palace was the primary summer residence of the Habsburg rulers. The 1,441-room palace is one of the most important architectural, cultural, and historical monuments in the country. The history of the castle and its vast gardens spans over 300 years. It was Laszlo's campsite for his second night away from home.

"I slept in the park. The next morning, I woke up, had breakfast, and hitchhiked to the German border. I was headed to a refugee camp there. When the border guard checked my passport, he saw that I didn't have a visa to enter Germany and wouldn't let me pass, so I spent the night in the Salzburg train station before I hitchhiked back to Vienna. I then caught a train to the refugee camp in Traiskirchen, which was 20 miles southwest of Vienna. I showed them my passport, and they let me in."

Traiskirchen is currently the home of the largest refugee camp in Austria and one of the largest camps in the European Union. It was first used as a refugee camp in 1956 for Hungarian refugees who had left their country due to the Hungarian Revolution in November of that year. The Austrian government decided to host further refugees from around the world and this was Laszlo's home for ten days in 1987. His stay wasn't long. He was kicked out because he had been leaving the camp to go to Vienna. Refugees were not allowed to work. He was caught and told he had to leave.

He went to Vienna and got an apartment with a couple of newly found Hungarian friends. It was now time to find work.

"At the time, there were a lot of Hungarian-owned stores selling electronics in Vienna. Because the border was now open, busloads of Hungarians would go shopping each day. They would come to Vienna to spend big money on refrigerators, other appliances, and electronics. They would tie refrigerators to the tops of their cars or take them back on the bus. They were cheaper in Vienna, and these products were hard to get in Hungary. My job was to bring those people into the store. I would stand on the street, and when I'd see a Hungarian group, I would go to them and bring them into the store. They paid me a flat $40 a day. I got paid on Fridays, and by Sunday, I'd spent it all in a club!" Laszlo laughed at the memory.

"I also did other things to supplement my income. Eastern Europeans were known for stealing a lot. I started stealing. I don't know why, but stealing stuff just came naturally to me. You dress up nice, walk in the store, nobody looks at you, you speak some German, and they leave you alone. I had orders to fill. People would come up to me and give me their shopping list. I would get the items, and they would pay me half of the retail price. It was a bad thing to do, but it was fun. I was good at it. That was my supplemental income, which became my main income after a while. I was making so much money that, I'm like, 'I'm not going to work on the street anymore.'"

Laszlo spent nearly two years in Vienna. He applied for a U.S. visa through an organization that helped immigrants come to the U.S. The organization flew him to Washington D.C. He stayed there briefly before moving to New York. He found a place to stay and got a job working at a Polish roofing company.

"I learned Polish before English because those guys didn't speak any English."

After close to a year, Laszlo went back to Vienna and back to the business he had done before. He began to specialize in moving stolen audio CDs into Hungary.

"I already had a dealer from Hungary coming to buy CDs for a Hungarian music shop. Of course, all this high-quality stuff like Led Zeppelin, Pink Floyd you couldn't get in the East. It was valuable. When my U.S. green card was about to expire, I chose to come back to the U.S. to extend it."

When he returned to New York City, Laszlo bounced between several jobs until a friend told him about a doorman position at a building on 5th Avenue.

"I was looking for something that had benefits—a job with a retirement fund and a pension. My friend was working as a doorman, and some Hungarians owned that building, and most of the workers were Hungarian. It was hard to get in because nobody wanted to quit. People waited years for this kind of job because there was excellent pay and excellent benefits. For that time, the pay was almost $70k after tips. At Christmas time, tips were 10 to 15 grand in cash. A guy quit, and they called me. I was fortunate to get in. It was a good job."

Laszlo had been working the door for six months when he met Agi.

"When I saw Agi, I just liked her. She was Polish. I spoke Polish because of the roofing job I had when I first came to New York. She was somebody different. "

Agi does not recollect if the attraction was instantaneous.

"He had to ask me several times to go out with him before I said, 'yes.'" Agi explained. "I wasn't looking for anything serious. Just fun."

Agi had her own journey to that spot in front of that building at that time to meet her husband. Agi was from Radom, a small city located about 60 miles south of Warsaw in central Poland.

"It was 1993 in Poland. I had finished school and was not ready to get a real job. I didn't want to be stuck in a classroom teaching in Poland," Agi recalls. "There was just more to life that I wanted to experience. I was with my friend, and we were saying that maybe we should experience what America was all about. So we applied for a U.S.visa. It was extremely difficult to get at the time. I spoke English at the interview, which I think helped a lot, and I got the visa! Then I had to get some money for the ticket because I wouldn't ask my parents for anything. At the time, a lot of people were going to Norway. I went there and worked as a housekeeper for a family. I made enough money for a plane ticket. My friend Ula was already living in New Jersey and working as a babysitter in Manhattan. She was pregnant and was looking for somebody to replace her. She told the family about me, and they called me in Poland. I interviewed and got the job. I already had a job waiting for me before I had even left!"

Agi bought a one-way ticket to New Jersey.

"I have four brothers, and I'm the only girl. My father kept saying that his girl was leaving him and that since he would never come to America he would never see me again. He felt like I was leaving him. But my father and my whole family were supportive, and they were proud that I had never asked for any money and that I had made my own plans. I just needed something more. It was in my head that I wouldn't stay in Poland."

Laszlo and Agi dated for several months after their meeting at the door on 5th Avenue.

"After a while, Laszlo moved in with my friend, Magda, and me in a two-bedroom apartment. I think it was like we were just dating, but I never thought, in my heart, that he was the one. It was just fun. I think that Laszlo fell in love with me sooner than I did with him. He showed me his heart. I saw my father in Laszlo. My father believed in family first and was a gentle, loving man."

Agi's green card was about to expire which meant that she would have to go back to Poland. Many people arranged marriages with U.S. citizens or other green-card holders just for the papers to stay in the country legally. Laszlo offered Agi such a deal.

"I offered that if she wanted to stay in the U.S., that I would marry her with no strings attached. It was a casual conversation. I just said, 'I like you. If you want to stay here I will marry you since I have my green card.'"

Agi smiled as she recollected the proposition. "It was just an arrangement, and we already lived together. I never felt like I owed him anything. We were boyfriend and girlfriend. We weren't strangers."

"So, we decided to get married in '95," Laszlo said. "Ironically, when we were first going out, I remember her saying to me, 'I'm never going to be your wife. We're never going to be together.'"

Love has a way of sneaking into hearts. A relationship that began with the simple act of opening a door, was sealed with an arranged proposition that established a relationship for a lifetime. Soul mates now married for over twenty-five years, they have two daughters, and there is no end in sight to their loving relationship.

"I can always count on him. He is always there for me. He's just so loving. To this day, I always know he is my pillar. He is the one."

LEAVE A 1-CLICK REVIEW!

I would be incredibly thankful if you could take just 60 seconds to write a brief review on Amazon, even if it's only a few sentences.

TELL YOUR STORY

WWW.WELOVETHATSTORY.COM

Tell us your story

What is the one story that has defined your life? If you would like to tell it, we are here to write it. This service is entirely **FREE**. All we want to do is share it with the world!

STEP ONE

Tell us who you are and how to contact you

Name:
Email:
Phone:
When is the best time to contact you:

STEP TWO

Title and Short Description

If you were to give your story a title, what would it be:

Provide a brief description of your story:

STEP THREE

Send your information

Email to jboglino@welovethatstory.com

THERE IS NO CHARGE FOR THIS SERVICE. YOU WILL RECEIVE YOUR STORY IN A WRITTEN FORMAT, AND IT MAY BE CHOSEN FOR ONE OF OUR SUBSEQUENT PUBLICATIONS TO SHARE WITH THE WORLD. WE ONLY ASK THAT YOU SIGN A RELEASE TO LET US PUBLISH YOUR STORY.

ACKNOWLEDGMENTS

I first figured out that everyone has a story to tell when my girl-friend, now my wife, and I were walking in a park in Krakow, Poland.

We saw an older man sitting on a park bench feeding the pigeons. I looked at my girlfriend and told her that we should approach and speak with him. I needed her because, at the time, I spoke only survival Polish. My girlfriend was my translator. We went up to the man, and he welcomed us to a seat beside him on the park bench. Two hours later, we had learned about his harrowing fight against the Nazis in 1942 in the Tatra Mountains in southern Poland. From that day, I was inspired and determined to find and tell stories. I don't want these individual tales to be lost to the passage of time. Since that moment, I have been drawn to connecting with people and learning from their experiences; I am committed to sharing their stories of hope, survival, success, and rebirth. I am very grateful for each person's time and vulnerability when recollecting times that may not have been the best. I hope these stories have a positive impact on my readers' lives, as they have on mine.

I have to thank my family for being my biggest cheering section. There would have been no way I could have pursued my dream of telling people's stories without their love and support.

Amy DeWitt has been my reviewer since the very first book that I wrote with another Peace Corps Volunteer in 1993. That effort, Where the Devil Says Goodnight, was a publication and guidebook about the southern region in Poland that transformed my life. While that was my rookie effort, I enjoyed writing every page with my Peace Corps friend, Kirk Henwood. We learned so much about the history of the area, what it went through after World War II and how it was emerging from the Iron Curtain in the early 1990s. Amy, another Peace Corps Volunteer at the time, was forcibly volunteered to edit that book, and she just made it better with her insight and English writing ability. I have been very thankful for her time and care for the stories that I am trying to articulate. She helps make sense of it all, and her input has been invaluable.

ABOUT THE AUTHOR

Joseph Boglino has been collecting stories his entire life. Inspired by the stories his mom and dad would tell him as a child, Joseph has been on a mission to elicit people's stories of overcoming challenges and finding strength. He hopes that by sharing these stories, the messages of hope and compassion will not be lost to the world but will instead thrive and inspire generations. After graduating with a degree in journalism from the University of Northern Colorado, Joseph joined the Peace Corps and served his two-year commitment in Poland. In a small town, Ustrzyki Dolne, he began collecting his first stories from people who lived through World War II and communism in Eastern Europe.

Joseph lives in the Denver area with his wife, Ania, and their three children, Kaj, Joshua, and Kalianna.

Printed in Great Britain
by Amazon

69676917R00085